D1592388

Patton's GI Photographers

Patton's
GI
Photographers

Edited by RALPH BUTTERFIELD

 Iowa State University Press/Ames

Ralph Butterfield was a member of the 166th Signal Photo Company, 89th Division, Third United States Army. After training at Camp Crowder, Missouri, he joined Patton's Third in England. He held a M.A. degree from Claremont McKenna College. He lived in Riverside, California, with his wife Elizabeth until his death in 1990.

Prior to his death, Ralph Butterfield made every effort to communicate with members of the 166th Signal Photo Company whose works are included in this book. Those he was able to locate have granted their permission for their work to appear in *Patton's GI Photographers*. There were a few, however, whom he was not able to locate. The publisher will be happy to include acknowledgments of these individuals in subsequent printings of this book.

Material by Russell A. Meyer has previously appeared in *A Clean Breast*, © Russell A. Meyer, and is reprinted here with Mr. Meyer's permission.

© 1992 Iowa State University Press, Ames, Iowa 50010
All rights reserved

∞ Printed on acid-free paper in the United States of America

No part of this book may be reproduced in any form or by any electronic or mechanical means, including information storage and retrieval systems, without written permission from the publisher, except for brief passages quoted in a review.

Authorization to photocopy items for internal or personal use, or the internal or personal use of specific clients, is granted by Iowa State University Press, provided that the base fee of $.10 per copy is paid directly to the Copyright Clearance Center, 27 Congress Street, Salem, MA 01970. For those organizations that have been granted a photocopy license by CCC, a separate system of payments has been arranged. The fee code for users of the Transactional Reporting Service is 0-8138-0216-4/92 $.10.

First edition, 1992

Library of Congress Cataloging-in-Publication Data

Patton's GI photographers / edited by Ralph Butterfield.—1st ed.
    p. cm.
    ISBN 0-8138-0216-4 (alk. paper)
    1. United States. Army. Signal Photo Company. 166th—History. 2. World War, 1939–1945—Photography. 3. World War, 1939–1945—Regimental histories—United States. 4. World War, 1939–1945—Campaigns—Western. 5. World War, 1939–1945—Personal narratives, American. 6. War photographers—United States—Biography.
I. Butterfield, Ralph.
D810.P4P38   1992
940.54′1273—dc20   92–5229

MEAD LIBRARY
SHEBOYGAN, WISCONSIN
9000714622

714622

Contents

Foreword

Every war has its chroniclers, in most cases people who write from the original experiences and accounts of others, and who insert analysis and personal opinion. Often these stories are quite good, as those accomplished by writers like Bruce Catton, Hubert Howe Bancroft, and Barbara Tuchman. Perhaps more compelling are the accounts written by individuals who participated in the event, because such works normally tend to be simpler and more authentic. The eminent historian Thomas Carlyle wrote: "Experience is the best of schoolmasters; only the school-fees are heavy." Oscar Wilde said the same thing in other words: "Experience is one thing you can't get for nothing."

In his book *Patton's GI Photographers* author/editor Ralph Butterfield has taken the best tack. He might have researched war records and photo collections from the usual primary sources in the National Archives and other places and coalesced them into a readable volume. He has done better than that. He has collected brief essays composed by his army buddies not long after combat, along with some very graphic photos shot by these men in action. The several texts, thirty-six in number, have the ring of authenticity because the authors were on the spot when things were happening. Properly, they tell their own stories in their own words. None of the stories were penned immediately following combat. The shelling was too intense, the noise too distracting, and the demands too severe. Also, the photographers continually were on the move. At Butterfield's suggestion, the accounts were written in camp near Marseilles in the weeks following the atomic bombing of Hiroshima and Nagasaki. This was about one year after the Allied landings on Utah and Omaha beaches in Normandy, but the cataclysmic experiences of war were yet fresh in the minds of the GI writers. As suggested by the maxims quoted above, the combat photographers gained their experience the hard way, and their work is the better for it.

The men whose stories and photos appear in this book were members of the 166th Signal Photo Company, a part of the 89th Division, Third United States Army. Its commander, the flamboyant, hard-charging Gen. George S. Patton, was one of the ablest if controversial military leaders of World War II. Early on, in April 1943, the 166th was activated at Camp Crowder, Missouri, and after basic training personnel were organized into photo teams and assigned to U.S. divisions overseas to record activities in bivouac and combat, mostly the latter. Members of the 166th joined Patton's Third Army in England in May 1944 after a brief training stint near Belfast, Ireland. It should be noted that these men were not ordinary GIs supplied with a camera and told to start shooting away. Most were people who came to the unit with considerable background in the field of picture making, as Sgt. Marvin Connell, who had been a set designer and photographer at the MGM Studios in California and Sgt. William E. Teas, who operated a professional photographic business in Pasadena, California, before the war. Others had similar experience with movie studios and the Eastman Kodak Company.

Private Howard Kuehne tells of "going to pieces" when German mortar shells blew men apart before his eyes. Actually, Kuehne did not fall apart until after taking pictures and helping medics tend the wounded. When the carnage became unbearable for this soldier he was evacuated to a field hospital in the rear. Pvt. Sam Gilbert tells an equally graphic story of the U.S. Fourth Armored Division's relief of Bastogne. There, in the numbing cold of an icy winter, Gilbert tells of seeing tree branches festooned with bits of human flesh, and frightened captive Germans being marched off to stockades in the rear.

Sgt. John Blankenhorn gives a vivid description of saturation bombing wherein the Allies employed two thousand B17 and B24 bombers and one thousand B26 planes to chew up an enemy-occupied area three thousand yards long and two thousand yards wide. So intense was the bombing that infantrymen were told they would walk into the territory "unscathed." Nothing could have been further from the truth. The approaches to enemy pillboxes were heavily mined with booby traps and antipersonnel devices, and as though that was not enough, "Kraut artillery" opened up and caused many casualties. Eventually the 243rd Armored Division broke through, but at considerable cost.

Sgt. Peter Anders relates of having a "grandstand seat" for the destruction of the German Seventh Army. Seated on a ridge overlooking the town of Chambois, he watched and photographed the whole thing. The devastation and carnage, according to Anders, was awesome. After the bombardment and shelling, sixty-seven thousand Germans lay dead upon the field of battle, strewn among dead horses, shattered equipment, and all of the melancholy debris of war. Wrote Anders, "Vehicles had to drive over [the bodies], flattening them into the dusty road until it looked like none were there."

Several of the photographers tell of the wild and unbridled enthusiasm exhibited by French people at the liberation of their towns and villages. On the happy side, exuberant Frenchmen swarmed aboard the U.S. tanks and half-tracks, waving flags, throwing flowers, showering kisses upon the tank crews, and plying soldiers with endless bottles of vintage champagne. On the dark side was the vicious treatment given to captured Germans and the revenge visited upon collaborators. Many of these were women, dragged away abruptly by the crowd to have their heads shaved as a mark of degradation and shame.

Some of the most compelling stories are those done by the author/editor of this book, Sgt. Ralph Butterfield. At Maizieres-les-Metz he was called upon to take photos of the 90th Division's reduction of the city. Holed up in a burned-out and shattered building of a steel foundry, he set up his Eymo camera and took his shots. German machine gunners peppered the building from a distance only yards away and mortars shelled the place from emplacements farther out. Later on, Butterfield and his teammate Russ Meyer took photos while perched high atop a railroad trestle in full view of the enemy. The battle raged for thirty days with 4.2 chemical mortars pounding the Germans along with a 155mm cannon. At the last, flamethrowers and hand grenades were used before hand-to-hand fighting took place. Butterfield was commended for the work he did at that time.

The story by Butterfield on his photographic assignment in Czechoslovakia at war's end is one of the best told here. The assignment was to photograph the return of President Eduard Benes in Prague after seven years in exile, and, if possible, to get a personal interview with the great man. Both tasks were accomplished, but only after difficulty in passing Russian checkpoints and fortuitous good luck with Czech nationals in Prague. Once in the city, the photo-team truck was guided to an up-front position in the great Town Square where photos of the Benes entourage could be easily taken. The photos taken here are outstanding.

Several days later, three American GIs, Butterfield among them, were ushered into the beautiful thirteenth-century Hradcany Castle on the banks of the Moldau River, ancient stronghold of the Bohemian kings. There, in a reception room with high-arched ceiling, huge chandeliers, and exquisite paintings, the Americans were received by the president. Benes gave a brief speech and ended it saying, "It is unfortunate that the West did not understand the wicked and evil intentions of the Nazis." Sergeant Butterfield answered saying that while a student at UCLA he had heard a similar assessment in a speech given by the Czech patriot Jan Masaryk. This pleased Benes who replied, "I too spoke at many of your universities in America. I shall not forget the kindness shown to me in your country."

It is of interest to note that the half dozen or more signal photo companies activated for overseas service during World War II are fairly well documented and that their exploits are sometimes mentioned in histories of the war. Thus records of achievements of these units are available in good libraries everywhere. Until now none of the histories have included the exploits of the 166th Signal Photo Company. Ralph Butterfield has performed a valuable service in bringing the very special contributions of the 166th to light. I recommend this book highly to all who are interested in this most remarkable period in our national history.

Riverside, California **—Cornelius Smith**

Preface

In huge tent cities sprawled across the white plains of northern France, thousands of American soldiers were billeted during July, August, and September of 1945. Transported from defeated Germany, they awaited redeployment.

In Camp New Orléans, the men of the 166th Signal Photo Company were expecting orders to proceed to Marseilles, where their equipment had preceded them, and to embark for the Pacific and the attack upon Japan. With the atomic bombing of Hiroshima on August 6, Nagasaki on August 9, and the surrender of Japan, Pacific-bound apprehensions gave way to homeward-bound elation. However, life in the camp continued with unchanged monotony, three months in all, scored weekly upon the outside of tents with chunks of chalk picked up from underfoot.

The boring inactivity suggested the opportunity for men to write, while relatively fresh in their minds, their experiences photographing events of the Third Army. Writing commenced with initial skepticism, mollified by my pledge that everyone in the outfit would receive a copy of what each man wrote. In their tents, seated upon cots, working with accelerated concentration, *Patton's GI Photographers* was written in about two weeks.

In camps adjacent to the 166th, several men, informed of the work in progress, became interested and provided invaluable assistance. After typing the material upon mimeograph stencils, they provided the services of a mimeograph machine operated by a German prisoner of war. Paper was provided by a dozen units, which in response to earnest scrounging filled the back of the jeep with packages. A friendly colonel signed the required security clearance upon the mailing envelopes, and the completed work was presented to each member of the company.

In the four decades that have passed since 1945, *Patton's GI Photographers* has become a document of historic significance, primarily because there is very little record about the 166th Signal Photo Company in the National Archives. Professor Peter Maslouski, who was writing about combat photography in World War II, noted, "I have been through many of the records kept by the Signal Photo Cos. that ended up in the National Archives—there's material there from the 161, 162, 163, 164, 165, 167, and 168, but not the 166."

A letter to me from Lt. Col. Harvey Weber explains the reason for the dearth of material on file: "Some mention was made by somebody about how scarce records (army) are on the 166th. It comes to mind that the company's equipment, records, belongings, etc., had been shipped to Marseille for trans-shipment to the Pacific when the war ended, and all of it disappeared into oblivion, never to be heard of again. I'm sure some Frenchman has got a lot of stuff marked ASSC. As nothing ever resurfaced, nothing ever ended up in the archives."

Many of the photographers ended up in careers similar to their army specialty. Don Ornitz became a nationally renowned photojournalist during the 1950s, his photographs appearing as multipage features in *Life* magazine, and other major publications. Russell Meyer has achieved national and international stature for his series of films, with constant accolades for their trend-setting and technical importance. He credits his training at Camp Crowder by Captain Arthur Lloyd for his mastery of the basics of cinematography. Aaron Lubitsch, who vividly described action at Cherbourg, has had a successful career with his photo studio in Wilmington, Delaware. He became a favorite of the governor of Delaware because of his photographic documentary series about the state. The most severely wounded in the first casualty of the 166th, Sam Sloan spent months in the hospital following amputation. He later built a large, diverse photography business, left it to his siblings, and retired to Florida.

Billy Newhouse, who found his high school friends in a prisoner-of-war camp in Moosburg, Germany, ended up in a career unrelated to his army experiences. An entomologist, he managed several enormous farms in the central valley of California. Marvin Connell, who described the Normandy breakout, returned to his specialty of set design at MGM Studios, a profession he had learned as a graduate in architecture from the University of Southern California.

Soldiers of World War II referred to themselves as GIs. The initials were derived from "Government Issue," the military designation for standardized equipment and procedures. The nickname was self-applied, a good-humored appraisal by men that they were anonymous, expendable, and regimented. It ignored other characteristics of the GIs—that they were individualistic, courageous, and duty bound.

Initiative and self-reliance were everyday characteristics of GI photographers, assumed without comment. Many of the personal experiences recorded here occurred during actions that were historically decisive in Third Army battles; other events were inconsequential tactically but memorable personally. Altogether, they reveal the unpredictable juxtaposition of dangerous, exciting, dramatic, and tragic occurrences commonplace in the lives of soldier photographers.

August 1990   **—Ralph Butterfield**

Introduction

AT COMPANY headquarters a crew member of the indispensable photographic laboratory, Pvt. Richard Simon, relates a comprehensive account of the formation, training, travels, and historical accomplishments of the 166th Signal Photo Company.

The army needed photographers! This was a War Department call in the early part of 1942. Working photographers from the New York area became the nucleus of the 161st, 162nd, and 163rd Signal Photo Companies. In conjunction with the army, the Academy of Motion Picture Arts and Sciences, Metro-Goldwyn-Mayer Studio, and Eastman Kodak Company provided rudimentary photographic training to personnel of five additional photo companies, the 164th–168th. The companies provided the photographic record of the history-making events of World War II in various parts of the world.

From one such group came forty men: former studio workers, artists, businessmen, some with substantial photography backgrounds at MGM and Eastman Kodak. This group, which was transferred from enlisted reserve status to active duty on December 26, 1943, found themselves at Camp Crowder, Missouri, and two weeks later became the future cadre and backbone of the 166th Signal Photo Company.

It was at Camp Crowder on April 5, 1943, that the 166th was finally activated. At that time the company consisted of twenty-one officers and eighty-four enlisted men. The enlisted men had been going through basic and cadre training courses, and were ready to take over the company when the fillers arrived on June 2. These new men were then given their basic course and trained to fill the duties of the organization. At this time a group of additional photographers from the Signal Corps School in Astoria, New York, joined the company, making the table of organization complete.

Soon after, the company photo laboratory set up, and the motion picture cameramen were given added combat photography instructions by army pictorial officers who conducted classes until early September 1943—when the majority of the company was ordered to Tennessee for military training on maneuvers. The various motion picture and still photographers were broken up into photo teams and assigned

to the various divisions to record all important division activities photographically. Other units of the company were sent to divisions in four
states: Wisconsin, South Carolina, Oregon, and Colorado. Their job
was to cover the divisions in training at camps. With these assignments well done, the company returned to Camp Crowder in November 1943 and prepared for overseas and the work for which they had
been so ably trained.

On February 26, 1944, the 166th boarded a naval ship, the *Susan
B. Anthony,* in New York Harbor and sailed for the European theater of
operations (ETO). On March 9, 1944, the convoy reached Belfast,
Northern Ireland. For the next two months, the company went
through more training and was quite impressed with the old manor at
Groomsport where they were billeted. It was there that they were first
assigned to the Third United States Army. The final photo units were
worked out of Groomsport, and all were readied for active service.
Then on May 6, the company left for England, the units being assigned
to all Third Army divisions and corps, and the laboratory and company headquarters setting up in two houses in a village near the city of
Manchester. The photo units became acquainted with their divisions,
and the laboratory set up to do a limited amount of work. One unit was
assigned to Third Army headquarters and covered all the happenings
of General Patton and his staff. Soon after, the laboratory received an
air corps trailer and moved their entire lab into this mobile unit, enabling them to process film during the entire campaign while on the
move.

When the invasion came on June 6, 1944, First Detachment (a six-
man unit consisting of two motion picture men, one still man, one
clerk, two drivers, and one officer) was preparing with the 79th Infantry Division to land on the invasion. The division hit the beaches on D
Day plus 6—the first unit of the company with them   and started on a
long combat mission ahead. The other photo units soon followed suit,
landing in France with every Third Army division and photographing
every phase of the great Normandy beachhead.

The company headquarters and laboratory, complete with trailer
and equipment, landed with Third Army headquarters on Utah Beach,
D Day plus 28, and moved directly into their bivouac area in Nehou,
France, to begin operations immediately. It was at this area on July 22
that news of the first battle casualties was received. An officer and a
sergeant from a unit with the 90th Infantry were killed while on a
photographic mission with the division. Two other members of the
unit were seriously wounded.

During the entire ETO campaign every important Third Army
event was photographed by the men of the 166th. Every division and
corps attached to the Third Army had a photo team operating with
them continuously—most units working from Normandy through Germany without a break or rest period. This was not an easy task to
accomplish—a task which was changing continually. During the Bulge
breakthrough, the Moselle crossing, and other such times when Third
Army received additional divisions and corps, photo teams had to be
assigned to them. The company, on the other hand, received no addi-

tional personnel, and so the original six-man teams were broken down into two- and three-man units, and by training the clerks and drivers as still men, the necessary quotas were met. The two men assigned to a division covered all the combat activities, drove their own vehicles, captioned their own work, and accomplished all that six had done before. The results of these units were more than satisfactory. The men, well trained in combat, did their job well and praise came in continually from all divisions.

The laboratory processed film day and night, moving practically once a week—never stopping work, except while actually moving from field to field. There was no water, so the necessary three hundred gallons needed for processing had to be hauled each day. A generator for added power due to ever-increasing work was provided and had to be checked out continually. Under practically every inconvenience imaginable, the lab turned out an average of twenty-eight thousand prints each month—a figure greatly exceeding any previous expectations. These included maps each night, which proved invaluable to headquarters while on the move.

The work processed in the company lab was that which was needed in the field for immediate technical and tactical value to the commanding generals of the army, corps, and divisions—since time would not permit the work to be returned to Company Z for processing. On the other hand, the Army Pictorial Service processed the rush news stories for release to publications in the States. Daily, all the unit news shots were rushed by plane to London and in turn radioed to the States, thus enabling any front-line shots to appear in a U.S. newspaper within forty-eight hours of the time they were taken. During the ETO campaign a total of three hundred thousand pictures were sent to Army Pictorial Service by units of the 166th—a permanent record of all Third Army historical events.

Motion picture film was handled in the same manner as the rushed stills. They were flown daily to London and then to the States for newsreel showing. An average of twenty thousand feet of footage was shot by the 166th units each week—a moving record of the Third Army that will live forever.

Attached to company headquarters was a two-man mobile camera repair unit which did all the repairing of damaged cameras, keeping each unit's equipment in perfect condition throughout the war.

The 166th men distinguished themselves above and beyond the call of duty. This group may well be one of the most decorated companies in the ETO. To date the awards for such service include fifty-five Bronze Stars, two Silver Stars, thirteen Purple Hearts, one Air Medal, one Legion of Merit, and one Croix de Guerre. Units have received individual division commendations and one unit with the 4th Armored Division was cited in the Presidential Citation to that division. This record speaks louder than any written praise as to the bravery and efforts of the men who make up the company.

Briefly that is the story of the 166th. Its photographic accomplishments are too lengthy to mention in entirety. It might be said that practically no newspaper, magazine, or newsreel has not at some time used pictures shot by a 166th cameraman. A special word should be added about the outstanding coverage of the German concentration camps by the 166th men. Pictures by them have brought to the minds of the world, better than by any other means, the horror and madness of the Nazi regime. More coverage on this subject was made by the Third Army units than by any other army and received grand-scale acclaim in the States and England. War crimes, too, have accomplished much with the aid of photo teams, as have the men in charge of photographing the tremendous numbers of German prisoners of war.

But first and foremost in the minds of the photographer was the thought of bringing a true combat picture of the war to all of the world. That is why the men had to go with the infantry, advance with reconnaissance patrols, and live at the front continually: to bring the stirring picture of the 4th, 6th, and 10th Armored and the unforgettable hardships of the 2nd, 4th, 5th, 26th, 35th, 65th, 76th, 80th, 90th, 95th, and all of the other famous Third Army divisions to every publication throughout the world.

Perhaps the story of the 166th can be best expressed in a letter General Eisenhower received from Mr. Walter Ament, chairman of the Newsreel Pool, New York, in which briefly he says:

> *I have been asked by all of the American Newsreel editors to extend to you our congratulations and thanks for the magnificent coverage of the Western Front combat activities accomplished by the U.S. Army Signal Corps cameramen under your command. Our appreciation for the quality of their work, and our admiration of their courage, could not be overstated. Without these service cameramen, the American public would have been deprived of a large proportion of the vitally important week-by-week newsreel presentation of the war in Europe. Our own correspondents, our staffs here at home, and the people of the United States owe them a great debt. I hope it will be possible for you to pass this message of appreciation to these brave and skillful men.*

—Private Richard Simon

I

THE PHOTOGRAPHERS who wrote in 1945 did so in camp near Marseilles, recalling vivid memories of recent experiences.

D Day plus 6, and Cherbourg

IN NORMANDY, as the Omaha and Utah invasion beaches became taxed to capacity landing men and material, the need for the port of Cherbourg became paramount. The 79th Infantry Division landed on D Day plus 6, a detachment of the 166th with them. Sgt. Aaron Lubitsch, a naturalized American who had emigrated from Russia as a young man, wrote as he spoke, with bursts of intense, enthusiastic sentences.

When on June 25 we looked down at the city, we knew the great port would soon be ours. From Fort Du-Roule, taken at early morning after a bloody fight, Colonel Robinson, commander of the 314th Regiment, 79th Infantry Division, pointed out the pillboxes.

"These," he said in a tired voice, "will have to be destroyed before we dare to come down the hill." The bombing plus the artillery had left these fortifications intact, and it was up to the doughboys to do the job—a job that was bloody and hard.

Loaded with camera and film, I tried to descend the hill with the First Platoon but got pinned down. Behind every burning building, a machine gun or burp gun was covering the approaches to the city.

"We'll have to burn them out," the platoon leader remarked. To "burn them out" was only a phrase. The platoon leader actually meant fight them and kill them.

I found a clearance in the wooded hill overlooking the railroad yard, and from there had a front seat for the show. The afternoon fighting on June 25 was a failure. We fought on the approaches, were held up, lost much, and decided to wait for more support. That night was a night of sweating it out. "Tomorrow," said Colonel Robinson, "the show will start, and it won't be play. There will be blood."

Zero hour was 0600. The artillery kept up for thirty-five minutes. The city became a huge ball of flame as though everything in it was afire. We made our way toward the railroad yard where we encountered our first stiff opposition. There were machine guns behind us and their fire was covering the whole area.

An army photographer is a soldier. No matter what happens in front of his eyes, he is not supposed to get too disturbed. He must keep an objective viewpoint, select salient action, and concentrate upon the technical matters of exposing or focusing. So I was calmly filming the scene as the platoon leader yelled, "Come and get the bastards!" Calmly? I was actually shaking like a leaf. I was scared. But once a man is in the thick of it, he forgets about his fear. He discovers it after he catches his breath.

Three men were lost in clearing out the machine guns, but the hard job had just started. There was a pillbox a couple hundred yards ahead of us and it had to be "burned out." Baker Company on our right flank had just been shooting up the works without actually fighting. Being nearest the pillbox, they were ordered to attack. There was one method of burning them out that employed a long stick with dynamite which had to be thrown into the pillbox from close range. "Long Jack," a tall guy from Arizona, was to carry the stick. "I'll get those bastards," he assured us, crawling toward the pillbox. But a couple of bursts of machine gun fire turned him back. It was too dangerous to try again, and it was decided to use artillery.

Fifty yards in front of the pillbox, the platoon leader of the First Platoon acted as forward observer, directing the fire. The first shell landed just beyond the target, the second clipped the side of the pillbox, and the third shell was a bull's-eye. This bull's-eye was the death of four Germans and a woman. These "morale" women were everywhere with the German troops.

There were a couple more entrenched strong points in the street before our objective, which was a corner building. But the Germans and their women didn't want to die. The day was much too beautiful, and no one wanted to see the sun for the last time—but many of our boys never did see the sun again. Slowly, we and other units on our flank were advancing through the narrow streets. Rifle fire echoed all over the town; Germans were still holding out. The stationed Cherbourg Garrison was still fighting and did not surrender until the waterfront was taken—until everything was covered in flames.

Cherbourg. For the army it was a triumph; for the photographer, blood and death in front of the camera viewfinder; for the weary GI, the largest liquor cache. "If I'd known there was so much liquor," Long Jack told me, a little on the happy side already, "I'd have gotten those bastards a long time ago!"

—Sergeant Aaron Lubitsch

THE PHOTOGRAPHIC DUTIES commenced when photo teams of the 166th Signal Photo Company, attached to various divisions, landed in France in the days after the invasion. The storm of high winds and rough seas that plagued D Day on June 6 subsided the following week. Dozens of ships departed from English ports on June 14, converged into a convoy, and landed at Omaha Beach in Normandy.

Sgt. Barney Caliend

FLOATING SIDE BY SIDE when they reached the shore, the LCTs rested on the sand with the receding tide, ready for debarkation. To some ships were tethered barrage balloons. They prevented strafing by enemy aircraft while crossing the Channel and upon the shore.

WITH A CONVENIENT ASSIST *by a bulldozed sand ramp, trucks drove directly from the craft, across the beach, and onto roads leading to inland France. The cavernous landing craft tanks transported tons of supplies, hundreds of vehicles, and thousands of soldiers. Over two hundred LCTs supplied the invasion, plying between English ports and the beaches.*

Sgt. Barney Caliendo

First Casualties, August 12, 1944

THE DANGER, the prospect, the price of a photographic mission was brought to the realization of each photographer when a mortar shell killed two and wounded two of a seven-man unit. Pvt. Howard Kuehne tells of the fatality.

This is the story of the Seventh Detachment of the 166th Signal Photo Company. It was a fine group of men, but was doomed to a short combat life.

We arrived on Omaha Beach on July 7, 1944, and after a short sojourn with the company headquarters at Nehou, France, we were ordered to report to Eighth Corps at La Haye-du-Puits. We spent some time at corps doing behind-the-lines work—until the attack to break the Saint-Lô–Perrier Highway was started.

The big drive was scheduled for August 12, and early that morning we drove down to the front on the right flank of the 90th Infantry Division. None of us had any previous combat experience, so we were all slightly nervous but in good spirits. The vehicle, being a command car, was left about a mile and a half back of the lines in a field, as the enemy had observation of anything larger than a jeep when closer. We caught a ride on a jeep to the forward command post and checked in for information. After obtaining the necessary briefing, we proceeded to a narrow roadway between two hedgerows to await the start of the attack.

Four tanks were firing from this position, and our artillery was located in the field above the road. We were in this roadway about three-quarters of an hour when the lieutenant asked us to come closer to him so he could tell us something. We never learned what it was, as almost immediately the Jerries started a searching barrage. We all hit the dirt, hugging the bottom of the hedgerow as close as possible to avoid fragments from the fields. I was on the end of the line closest to the Jerry lines, and about five feet separated me from our officer, Lieutenant Shadden. Sergeant Richmond and Tech. Sgt. Walker were about seven feet farther down from him, and Private Sloan seven feet past them.

Suddenly, in the middle of the noise, there was a roar and a shock that stunned me for a short time. As I began to get my bearings and move to see if I had been hit, I heard Walker and Sloan cry for help. I turned as I got up and started toward them. A pack on Sergeant Richmond's back was burning due to shrapnel hitting the inflammable film he had placed in it. I cut it loose . . . . [The lieutenant and another GI, Sgt. Rasmussen, were already dead.] Walker had been riddled with shrapnel and Sloan also. Sloan was the worst of the two as shrapnel had smashed his right leg between the ankle and the knee and also struck him in the back. As I attempted to administer first aid, I called for stretcher-bearers and after what seemed hours—but was most likely minutes—they appeared.

We carried the two men out and then went back for the camera equipment. Because the mortar barrage was still going on, I could only carry part of it at once. When I got ready for the second trip, one of the fellows from the aid station went with me. We checked the lieutenant and sergeant to make sure we could not help them and then carried the rest of the stuff back. By this time the two injured men had been evacuated, so I started back with the cameras. After walking a mile or so, I caught a ride on a jeep to regimental headquarters. Our vehicle and driver were not there, so I left the cameras and started after him along another road towards the front. After finding him we both went back, picked up the cameras, and returned to the company.

The reaction then set in and I went to pieces. I was sent to the 101st Evacuation Hospital nearby for treatment of shock. There it was discovered that only a tiny piece of shrapnel had entered my back, though I had been but five feet from the exploding shell.

—Private Howard Kuehne

Sgt. Barney Calien

THESE MEN were probing for land mines. German vehicular mines detonated under pressure of 250 pounds or more. The overturned jeep was destroyed by one, and the occupants killed.

On both sides of the road are hedgerows, centuries-old compact masses of roots and stones topped with dense thickets. When hedgerows enclosed fields, as in the bocages regions of Normandy, they were very difficult to penetrate and were stubbornly defended by the Germans in June and July of 1944.

Lt. Adrien Salvas

FOUR GIs substitute for medics as they carry a wounded comrade to an aid station.

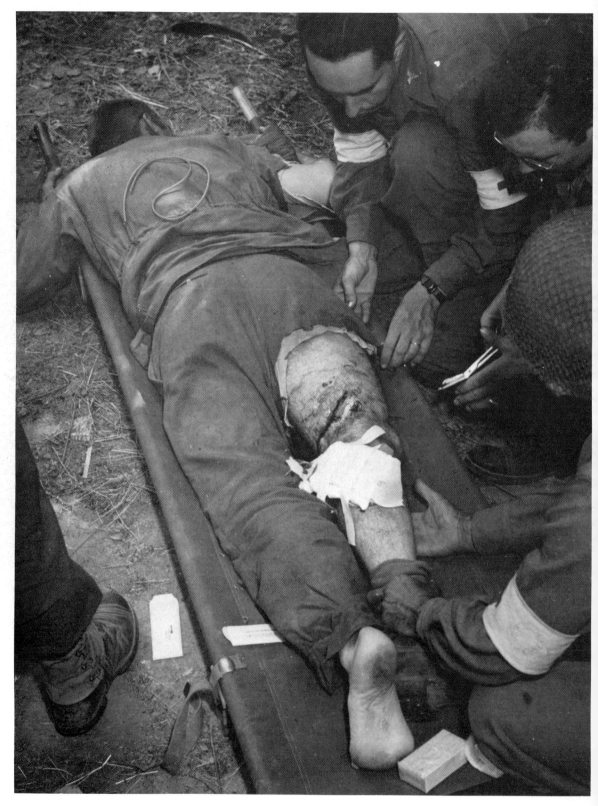

Lt. Adrien Salvas

A WOUNDED SOLDIER is given first aid.

Sgt. Barney Caliendo

GRAVES REGISTRATION UNITS *performed the sad duty of removing
the men killed in action from the battle sites.*

INFANTRYMAN: *(Angrily, with his rifle pointed at the photographer)* "Hey, lay
off. Don't take that picture. My buddy is in that truck."

PHOTOGRAPHER: *(Heatedly)* "Wait a minute! I'm tired of taking pictures of
guys in tanks and artillery firing. I want people at home to
see that men get killed in this war."

INFANTRYMAN: "Well, OK then . . . ."

Saturation Bombing

THE FIGHTING in Normandy was at close quarters and bitter, with massed artillery, tank-dozers, and infantry that dug the enemy out of holes burrowed in the banks of hedgerows. Bloated cattle in the fields were round and grotesque with legs pointed skyward. Ground haze held the odor of the dead for days. At Saint-Lô the fighting reached its climax, and with the tremendous saturation bombing at the last of July, the Normandy confinement began to break. Sgt. John Blankenhorn tells of this.

Toward the end of July 1944, the Allies—still penned up in Normandy—had enough power to attempt a breakthrough into the interior of France. With the aim of effecting this penetration, several special troop dispositions were organized, among which and probably most important was the Seventh Corps commanded by General Collins. Collins was one of the battle wise commanding generals, having served at Guadalcanal earlier in the war. This corps had as its area that ground immediately bordering the Nineteenth Corps, which was the unit attacking Saint-Lô. Just west of Saint-Lô was the town of Marigny, a road junction between Carentan to the north, Lessay and Periers to the west, and Coutances to the southwest. This town was held by the Germans, and Seventh Corps forces were about three miles from advancing from the south. The corps was made up from the 1st, 4th, and 9th Infantry Divisions and the 2nd and 3rd Armored Divisions. The 9th Detachment of the 166th Signal Photo Company was attached to the 9th Infantry Division.

The idea of the attack was to capture Marigny and break the 2nd Armored Division out onto the roads west—one to go to Lessay and the other to Coutances, thus trapping the German forces on the western end of the line. This was to enable the armored division of the Third Army to pass around the disorganized western end of the Germans and proceed both into Brittany and the interior of France.

As a prelude and, it was hoped, a decisive element in this attack, a large number of heavy bombers were to be employed for the first time in direct support of ground troops. Two thousand B17s and B24s and one thousand B26s were to come over in waves and drop bombs on an area three thousand yards long by two thousand yards wide, between Seventh Corps troops and Marigny—but not on the town itself. This was saturation bombing, and a possible hazard to the U.S. troops was foreseen and allowed for in that night preceding the day of the bombardment. Our troops withdrew one thousand yards. A retirement of this kind is most valuable if it can be achieved without the enemy's knowledge. But secrecy was considered to be a pretty forlorn hope in this instance as the Germans were maintaining close contact.

The briefing we received was to the effect that the bombing would last one hour and forty-five minutes and would be followed by a thirty-minute artillery barrage. After that was over, it would be possible to march unscathed into Marigny.

It started, I remember, at 11:45 with P47s going in after the "flak" guns, but when the heavies came over at 12:00 there were still a good many greasy black botches in and around them. One of the first planes was hit, and seeing it flounder got me in the pit of the stomach—the sort of sensation experienced if a great, friendly St. Bernard were to be hit by a car and not quite killed. It fluttered and struggled but the Jerries just waited until it lost altitude, and then the guns went all at once and the plane blew to pieces.

The noise of the bombs falling was monumental, not just an explosion or even a series of explosions but more like an earthquake trying to shake a city to pieces. The concussion stirred up a strong wind as far as four miles away and even at that distance made you feel a little nauseated. After about half an hour there was a wall of dust and smoke over four thousand feet high above the area.

We took off for the command post of one of the battalions to get ready to "walk unscathed into Marigny" when it was over. The bombing of course was still going on, and nearly everyone there had lost their lunch because of the horrible vibrations. I promptly lost mine too. The dust was unbelievable, and that plus the tension of sweating out some plane bombing us by mistake more than overcame any exultation we might have experienced at the Jerries getting such a pasting. The country was hedgerows at their worst, since it was hilly, the *bocages* especially tall, and the fields very small. The usual props were present: one-walled houses, demolished apple trees, and, as always, the cow—bloated and upside down. During the time we were at the battalion, two sticks of bombs fell short to one side of us and not far away. General McNair was one of the casualties.

At company, the sensation was infinitely worse and weird in appearance, in that GIs, radio sets, medics' arm bands, and dead cows were exactly the same color as the dust.

After the air bombardment, the barrage seemed childish and ineffectual. Everyone was getting up to move out on our "unscathed" walk. We moved out onto the road with the company commander and passed a tank destroyer (TD), which was firing at something we couldn't see. Our "walk" lasted about one hundred feet. After that we huddled "unscathed" in a ditch. German confetti came in by the ton,

supply lines were of unbelievable length and our infantry support was still closer to Omaha Beach than they were to us. The enemy didn't expect the unorthodox, but Wood got away with it in taking Rennes and Vannes and cutting the Brittany peninsula from the mainland, completing one of the longest armored dashes ever made in the face of the untried enemy.

Wood was given the name of Tiger Jack for his habit of pacing his tent in the manner of a caged tiger whenever his men were in combat. He advised his gunners to fire on anything that they suspected—thereby using 60 percent more ammunition than any other division. But with such phenomenal success across France by his 4th Armored Division, one of the most perplexing questions of the war remains: Why was General Wood replaced?

—Sergeant Marvin Connell

"BUT THE NOW-FAMOUS 4th PUSHED ON. Having the Germans on the run, our armor cornered the enemy at Avranches and left a mass of death and destruction as far as it was possible to see."

Sgt. Ralph Butterfield

Brittany and Brest, August 8

FREE TO MOVE unexpectedly, the 6th Armored Division penetrated southward behind the 4th, and then went westward into Brittany. Affiliated infantry and combat engineers fought in the towns, at the bridges, and in the woods. The enemy closed behind forward elements, and supply trucks bearing gasoline, rations, and communications equipment fought their way in both directions. The ports of Saint-Nazaire, Lorient, and Brest received thousands of German troops who withdrew before the American penetrations. These enemy troops were contained by a small number of tanks and "recons" who were on the "end of a limb" until infantry arrived to consolidate them. Private Hansel tells of his experience as he went to rejoin the division after it had made its run across Brittany.

On August 8 our photo unit of six men was ordered to join the 6th Armored Division on the tip of the Brest peninsula. At that time the 6th had finished its drive down the center of the peninsula. Since the drive employed no infantry other than the armored infantry of the division, the route they had opened had been closed behind them by the Germans. Over this same route the Quartermaster Truck Company had to haul gasoline and ammo. The only possible means of our reaching the 6th was to tie on to such a convoy. The afternoon of August 9 we met our convoy near Avranches, France. We waited until 1900 hours and then took off. We didn't know exactly what route we were taking, and little did we suspect that we were starting a 185-mile trip to Brest involving twenty-four hours of steady driving.

It was approximately 2200 hours when we encountered our first obstacle—a bridge that had been blown the day before. The three-mile-long convoy was completely turned around and rerouted. It was during this maneuver that our unit, along with the second half of the convoy, was separated from the leading element. Somehow we managed to get back on the right road and started out again. We drove continuously the rest of the night and up to ten hours on August 10, at which time our forward jeep ran into a Jerry machine gun nest. The four multiple-50s the convoy carried as a safety measure were spaced evenly along the line of trucks, and every man except drivers had guns fully loaded and ready for instant action. This was accomplished during a backtrack maneuver which led us to a little French town held a mile behind our line of march. There we turned around and—now more fully organized—again headed for the machine gun nest. When we reached the spot, not a shot was fired, and we rolled on to finally reach the comparative safety of the 6th Armored Division, which faced the Germans on three sides. One week later the full-scale Battle of Brest began.

—Private Hansel

Fortification Plans, Saint-Malo and Dinard

SAINT-MALO was at first bypassed, and when it was later besieged the fighting was limited by the ability of the cement fortifications to absorb heavy bombardment. Air attacks and artillery were ineffectual against the concrete. Tremendous explosions ripped off chunks of debris, but the defenders continued to hold. Sergeants Curry and Ryan were able to get into the town, and they were drawn into events beyond their mission.

In five days of hard fighting, two task forces of the 83rd Division had compressed the Germans on the Saint-Malo peninsula into the city of Saint-Malo on the tip. Surrounded on three sides by water, this enemy force could now throw its entire strength against the U.S. troops thrusting up to the peninsula.

A speedy seizure of the port was necessary to relieve overloaded Cherbourg and the impending immobilization of our beachheads by the coming September storms. Our lines were soon stabilized. After a two-day air and artillery preparation, the companies jumped off at daybreak, the objective being the city itself. By 0900 hours almost all companies had been halted by the heavy enemy artillery concentrations. As I and K companies on the left flank were making slow progress, we decided to join K. This decision proved to be correct, as K

Company entered the town at 11:15, the first unit in. Our job consisted of showing—in motion pictures and stills—our I and K companies entering the town down the dusty, shell-ploughed road, past badly battered buildings. It was a matter of dodging, running, and sweating.

As the spearhead split the enemy into small bands, it afforded pictures of Germans coming out of buildings to surrender. When an officer of the marines led his men out, shots fired by fanatics cut him down. Our boys advanced on this sniper point as several bursts from the Nazis pinned them down. Another burst cut down one of our BAR men, his ammo exploded, but the *boche* (German) continued to fire on him, cutting him to ribbons. The snipers' house was taken with five Germans inside.

When we were ready to start back, it was learned from the commanding officer of K Company that the Germans had succeeded in reforming their lines, thereby cutting the company off in town. The radio was out and we had no communications with the battalion. As we intended to try to make it back that night, the CO entrusted us with a message calling for reinforcements and medical supplies, which we were to deliver to battalion headquarters. Taking nearly an hour to work our way about a mile, we split to increase our chances of getting our message in when a German machine gun on our right opened up on us. After surviving a mortar barrage unscathed, we both made it into the battalion late that evening with the message.

In looking over our souvenirs, we discovered that we had picked up a case containing a map of the fortifications. The map indicated all German gun emplacements on both Saint-Malo and Dinard. This map was used by G-2 (military intelligence) and aided in the expeditious termination of the battle for Saint-Malo.

—Sergeants Robert Curry and James Ryan

SUPPORTING CONVOYS followed the tanks that pushed into France, southward to Rennes, and eastward to Brest. The Third Army, on the flank of American and British positions, was strategically located for General Patton's unique leadership of nonstop tank penetrations.

166th Signal Photo

Annihilation, Falaise Gap

BRITTANY was incidental to the principal Allied effort. Eastward the British fought in the north, and the Third Army drove a flanking movement in the south, threatening the German Seventh Army. The Germans attempted to escape through the Falaise Gap, and Sgt. Peter Anders witnessed the first major catastrophe of German resistance in France.

We went with the 90th Infantry Division on its drive north from Le Mans to get coverage of their push to meet the British coming from Caen, which would close the gap on the German Seventh Army attempting to withdraw to the Seine. The final junction was made at the town of Chambois, situated in a beautiful valley through which passed the only possible German escape route.

The 90th got the ridge overlooking the valley. It was like a front-row balcony seat at a theater. The weather was perfect for photography and the unobstructed view was magnificent. We set up the newsreel camera there and for five days covered the carnage and battle taking place at our feet. A highway ran along the lip of the ridge, on which antitank guns were set up for direct fire at a distance of not more than half a mile. They sighted down the barrel and then fired. All the artillery available was massed behind us. The Germans were plainly visible with the naked eye, desperately trying to figure their way clear.

On August 21 we tried to get into the village of Chambois with a patrol but were driven back. At 1:15 on August 22 we did get in and ran into four German tanks. We called for artillery, which came in a deluge and knocked out the tanks, but we were so close to them that we lost a lot of men also. With those tanks gone we cleared the village and drove to the far side, where we met the British elements of Canadian and Polish outfits. The Germans gave up as the last road was cut off.

In that area of the valley, within a radius of two miles of the village, were sixty-seven thousand German dead plus their shattered equipment, horses, and wagons. Fifty-four thousand were taken prisoner. This action at Chambois definitively removed the German Seventh Army from hostilities in Europe. (It was a newsreel man's dream.) Bodies were so numerous and so scattered it was impossible to care for them, and vehicles had to drive over them, pushing and flattening them into the dusty road until it looked as if none had been there. Bulldozers from the American army finally skimmed all bodies into ditches and covered them. Such action was the only recourse because of the overwhelming number and the summer heat.

Most vivid of my recollections were romantic young Frenchmen escorting their girlfriends on bicycle sight-seeing tours back and forth along the road on the ridge, which was under heavy shelling from the Germans, and across where we were firing—so they could see the spectacle in the valley below.

—Sergeant Peter Anders

A FRENCH WOMAN, unperturbed by the men bathing, shares a village laundry shelter with two GIs as they wash clothing beside a stream. Bathing was a luxury. For several weeks in July, as the tanks and half-tracks battered the roads, a pall of dust coated the men, clothing, and equipment in layers of grime.

Liberation, Reims

WHATEVER the fighting, wherever the village, town, or city, the exuberant, sincere, and demonstrative gratitude of the French people toward their liberators was universal. Tears and wine, flowers and cider mixed in unabashed joy for men in tanks and half-tracks, trucks, and jeeps when they passed between lines of cheering people. Corporal Sullivan, in entering Reims, found a welcome that all photographers experienced at one time or another.

Probably in none of the liberated cities of France was the carnival spirit more evident than when the 7th Armored Division roared into Reims on the heels of the retreating Jerries. This city, famous for its majestic cathedral of Notre Dame and well known for its excellent champagne, escaped most of the grim horrors of besiegement and block-by-block street fighting incidental to the freeing of so many French cities. The minor defending forces, dreading the impact of Patton's approaching armor and completely demoralized by the fantastic type of guerrilla warfare waged by the French Resistance, chose the better part of valor and left—that is, those whom the FFI (French Forces of the Interior) allowed to leave. The Resistance forces then promptly turned their efforts to cleaning up remaining snipers and rounding up *collaboratrices* (female collaborators) for the shaven-head treatment.

When the Americans entered the town, we were led by cheering, screaming, laughing mobs to the square in front of the cathedral. Here the vehicles were transformed into seething mounds of exuberant humanity as civilians, children, lovely girls, and even bearded men decided that he or she must personally embrace each and every American GI. It was here that one of our photo team was modestly suffering the caresses of a comely mam'sel when two smiling maquis approached and explained that she was a *boche collaborateur*. Whereupon, they marched her off for a haircut—leaving a very red-faced photographer.

Meanwhile, I had made the acquaintance of an American flier who, upon being assured the city was now in free hands, disclosed the presence of another Yank and three British airmen who had been in France for periods ranging from two weeks to four months. These men, after being shot down, had been rescued by members of the Resistance who furnished them with civilian clothing and faked credentials. They were transported from place to place by wagon, bicycle, oxcart, and what have you, to eventually arrive in Reims. There they stayed—living on smuggled food and champagne (mostly champagne) waiting for the Americans.

The impromptu spontaneity of our first reception was soon followed by a more formal ceremony at the *mairie* or city hall. There was much speech making and flash of colorful uniforms. The people jammed the streets, draped themselves all over the statue of Louis XIV, shouted "Vive l'Amérique!"—and reached for the nearest American.

Later in the afternoon we had an opportunity for a more leisurely look at the Notre Dame Cathedral. The massive doors were protected by thick cement walls and sandbags piled high around the statuary in front of the church. Inside all was quiet—the quiet of an ageless and unchanging refuge through war and peace for hundreds of years. There were American soldiers there, civilians too. For a moment they had forgotten the tumult outside—their minds on other things.

By evening most of the celebrating was indoors, for there was still danger from occasional sniper fire—either the snipers or patrolling maquis mistakenly shooting at each other. We were never quite sure of that. Early the next day the city was declared "Off Limits" for the American troops. The GIs had to leave, but they left with memories of beautiful girls and good champagne. An hour before we left we again met our friends, the liberated British and American pilots. This was at the Pomery Vinery. They were filling their borrowed jeep with cases of—all things—champagne.

—Corporal Charles Sullivan

Lt. Adrien Salva

FOUND LYING in the rubble and debris of a clothing store display window, "Mademoiselle" was momentarily restored to her modeling role by irrepressible GIs.

Lt. Adrien Salvas

FRENCH SCHOOLCHILDREN, standing upon a jeep and trium-
phantly displaying Nazi souvenirs, demonstrate with a rousing
liberation shout. Boys were fascinated with soldiering, frequently
wearing cast-off canteens and helmet liners. They recognized the
generous, friendly nature of American GIs. In England they requested, " 'ave you got any gum, chum?'' In France they wheedled,
"Cigarette pour Papa?"

Paris, Porte d'Orléans

THE LIBERATION of Paris would be a political and moral victory of world interest and attention. Representatives of all major news and publicity agencies attached themselves to the divisions approaching the city. With the first Allied troops to enter was Sgt. Russell A. Meyer and the 2nd Armored Division.

Accompanying the Second French Armored Division (Division LeClerc), I entered Paris on the morning of August 25 at 7:30 A.M. through the Porte d'Orléans, after two weeks of continuous driving. With me in the jeep was my photo officer, First Lt. E. J. Moore, Culver City, California; Cpl. C. E. Sumners, Vincent, Alabama; and Cpl. C. Sullivan of New York City.

Everywhere I looked there were pictures to be taken; people crowded the broad avenue, cheering and feverishly clutching at our clothing as we passed. The terrific congestion necessitated occasional stops at which time we were showered with embraces and kisses from the excited populace. Upon dismounting from the jeep I was barely able to take any pictures; people crowded around me expressing their appreciation. By then our jeep was loaded to capacity, which necessitated that we photographers ride on the hood of the vehicle. An amusing incident occurred at this point: I ripped a great hole in the seat of my trousers! This caused me no end of embarrassment for the remainder of the day.

Our vehicle was sandwiched between two of the lead tanks for protection. We halted and dismounted from the jeep at numerous intervals, whenever the snipers and Nazi sympathizers opened fire on us from the rooftops. The activities of the FFI and the French tanks cleaning out these snipers offered excellent motion picture and still coverage. In one instance when we turned down a side street in search of pictures, we were halted rather abruptly by a man that later proved to be an American citizen who had somehow hidden his identity from the Nazis for years. At first he considered us to be French soldiers due to the likeness of our dress and was overjoyed to learn that we were

Americans—the first that he had seen in many years. His timely action saved our lives; for as soon as he had greeted us he exclaimed, "For God's sake don't go down that street, it is full of Germans!"

Our activities for the remainder of the day were very much the same with plenty of excellent photographic opportunities. Our finest action pictures were gotten down on the Quai d'Orsay where French tanks encountered heavy antitank fire.

The people of Paris treated us handsomely; nothing was too good for us. We made several good friends, many who have been corresponding with us continuously. We had spent days living under the most extreme physical discomfort as well as danger, and most of all we enjoyed the hospitality of the fine Parisian family who took us to their home so we could bathe, sleep, and rest.

—**Sergeant Russell A. Meyer**

THE LIBERATION OF PARIS, the symbolic heart of France, was eagerly anticipated with worldwide interest, and especially by the enthusiastic Parisians. To the tanks of the French Second Armored Division was granted the privilege of leading the entry into the city and receiving the tumultuous welcome.

WHITE ARMBANDS *identify French civilian Resistance members, the FFI, as they escort a contingent of German prisoners through an unsmiling, sober crowd.*

Photo by Photo Presse Libération, courtesy of Sgt. Ralph Butterfield

The Snipers of Notre Dame, "Vive de Gaulle!"

THE FERVOR and furor of the liberated city was more intense the next day, when Gen. Charles de Gaulle led the victory procession from the Arc de Triomphe down the Champs-Élysées and through the Place de la Concorde to Notre Dame Cathedral. Here Sgt. William E. Teas, motion picture cameraman assigned to the Second French Armored Division that had liberated Paris, found himself in memorable occurrences.

The huge square in front of the cathedral was solid with sunlight and shouting Parisians eager to see and greet Gen. Charles de Gaulle. This was to be his official homecoming, as well as the welcome party for his soldiers returned triumphant from the humiliation of Dunkerque and the furtive, hunted escape routes through Spain and Vichy territory. France hung her tricolor heart along his line of march and milled about before her most famous religious shrine, waiting expectantly but far from silently.

The square began to overflow. Tanks of the Second French Armored Divison nudged gently but ineffectually at the bulging line of humanity bordering the cathedral steps, keeping the space clear for Generals de Gaulle, LeClerc, and Koenig.

Skirting the square and elbowing through the gathering fringe, the FFI interpreter and I slipped through the east gate of the cathedral wall, past the BBC apparatus, and into the cathedral proper.

Inside, the many frocked padres we approached with our request were vague but pleasantly adamant. There could be no permission to photograph the procession from the lofty tower: It was forbidden. I produced my credentials as an offical United States Army cameraman, and Jacques, my interpreter, argued in rapid French. The padres were sorry, but it was forbidden. Who forbade it? The police forbade it. . . . Merci.

Outside we sought and found a succession of rank in local gendarmerie. Following the chain of command well toward the bowl, we flushed an explanation. No one was to be permitted in the tower because there were Germans in the tower and they were armed and would probably fire on de Gaulle when he arrived.

This struck me as sheer fantasy and the most imaginative and disarming brush-off I had ever received. Deprived of the bird's-eye perspective, I busied myself with build-up shots of the crowd, the long line of mechanized honor guard, SP (self-propelled) artillery, and tanks and half-tracks with their red-capped spahi colonial troops.

The sergeant chiefs of the tank crews deployed nearest the cathedral were in pitched battle with civilians who insisted on clambering atop the vehicles for better vantage. The women were particularly persistent. One sergeant deserted his role of bellowing command for cajolery and please, "S'il vous plaît." There was derisive laughter and expressive noises not in the *Soldier's Phrase Book.* The tanks were hopelessly swarmed with bright dresses and serge of a nonmilitary shade. And that was that, and I doubt if Charles de Gaulle himself could have done anything about it.

I struggled to descend and had reached the rear of the tank when an abrupt cheer burst from the square, then a unison swelling cheer of "Vive de Gaulle!! Vive de Gaulle!!" Turning, I fought aloft to catch a fleeting glimpse of a decorated car rolling up before the cathedral.

At that moment firing began from somewhere. The cheering turned to screams of hysteria as kicking, panicky people scrambled off the trespassed tanks. I was thrown from the tank, trampled, and left without a camera, which the capable Jacques managed to rescue. As the firing from the cathedral increased and Moroccan soldiers spattered the front of the edifice with a spray of 50-caliber ammo, we were separated and I was left to observe one of the most emotional moments of history without a viewfinder.

Fortunately for all concerned, our other motion picture unit cameraman, Sgt. Ted Sizer, was filming the fleeing and huddled pedestrians, and the stalking, angry figure of General LeClerc, who was frantically waving his inimical cane at the machine guns. A fine mist of powdered limestone drifted earthward from the machine-gunned facade of the cathedral.

From Sizer we had the eyewitness account of de Gaulle's unperturbed march down the long carpeted aisle of the cathedral as the organ played the pompous strains of the "Te Deum" above the unbidden chant of the firearms. With no outward regard for shells ricocheting above or the crouching figures of police and FFI returning fire into the dim, dismal heights surmounting the altar, he proceeded with the ceremony just as originally planned.

Shortly the firing ceased, except for a few sporadic bursts of nuisance value, and Jacques and I found each other and Sergeant Sizer. I surrendered my build-up footage to Sizer with some hastily scribbled captions, reloaded the camera, and hung about hoping something would break.

People began coming out of the adjoining alleyways and doors and started to congregate boldly in the open square once again. Everyone was inquiring of each other if de Gaulle had been injured. The old cry of "Vive de Gaulle!" went up again for awhile—then the tenor of the shouting changed as the crowd discussed the event excitedly and became outraged at the perpetrators.

On a hunch I remounted my turret position in the event that de Gaulle or anyone else of consequence should emerge from the cathedral. Through the gate entrance nearest me came a struggling group of gendarmes with five prisoners they had routed from the tower. They wore civilian clothes with dark-rimmed glasses and looked very French—like overgrown students.

I started grinding as the crowd spotted them and went wild all over again. Desperately the gendarmes fought off the viscious, hurling attacks of the spectators, clinging doggedly to their charges and dragging them along. Someone among the police had enough foresight to pivot them down the palisaded stairs and along the quay of the Seine where it paralleled the square, avoiding the greatest part of the throng. The cry for blood mounted, and I thought for one cold moment that they were going to be lined up along the riverbank and executed on the spot. More gendarmes joined the struggle, and by the time they ascended the stairs adjoining the far side of the square the body had broken into three or four distinct groups, each guarded by a half dozen or so gendarmes.

The victims were pretty bloody by this time. The glasses were gone and they didn't particularly look French anymore. One of them was unconscious and was being dragged by his forelock, the press of the pursuers holding his limp body half erect. With effort, the huge doors of the *mairie* were pulled shut after the would-be assassins had been carried through. People milled about outside awhile and made a lot more noise which gradually diminished. Men breathed heavily with the exhaustion of the hunt, shook their heads, and smiled tensely at one another in acknowledgment of the strenuous experience shared. Out in the square, a French girl laughed. Over by the cathedral someone was starting the "Vive de Gaulle!" cry again. I leaned against an FFI sedan, sponged body sweat with my free hand, and tried to ignore the optimistic urchin asking for "Cigarette for Papa?"

Gradually, Paris remembered that she was celebrating her liberation, and the communal drinking started again in the streets below the desperate finale in which young Frenchmen clambered over the city's rooftops, seeking snipers in true thriller style.

We never knew the outcome of our brief moment in history, for censorship reared its unfathomable head. A brief but accurate account of the events of the attempted assassination crept by some device into *Time* magazine. But I doubt if there were any other correspondents or cameramen who by some peculiar device of fate had been told at least an hour before the shooting started that there were "Germans in the tower and they were armed and will probably fire on de Gaulle when he arrives."

—Sergeant William E. Teas

Sgt. William E. Teas

WITH JOYOUS GRATITUDE, enthusiastic Parisians greet liberation troops of the Second French Armored Division at Porte de Saint-Cloud, August 24, 1944.

Sgt. William E. Teas

WHILE A PARISIAN BOY rides upon an armored vehicle, young women warmly greet French soldiers on Liberation Day, August 24, 1944.

Sgt. William E. Teas

A PARISIAN BEAUTY seeks a personal conversation with one of her city's liberators, as he relaxes upon the hood of a jeep.

Photo by Photo Presse Libération, courtesy of Sgt. Ralph Butterfield

CIVILIANS, menacingly bitter toward their captives who had controlled their city during four years of humiliating occupation, energetically routed out many German soldiers.

Sgt. William E. Teas

DIGNITARIES on the reviewing stand during the liberation of Paris parade. From left: *the civilian mayor of Paris, an unidentified French officer, General de Gaulle, General Hodges, General Bradley, and an unidentified American officer.*

SOLDIERS *of the Polish troops assigned to the French Armored Division receive floral accolades during the liberation parade in Paris, August 1944.*

Sgt. William E. Teas

Seventh Army Linkup,
Lieutenant Eve Curie

WHEN the American Seventh Army invaded France in the south and fought up the Rhone Valley, the area between them and the Third Army was cleared for the most part by the FFI. Early junctions between the two forces were token ones, and Tech. Sgt. Warren Harding relates his experiences at a meeting.

While serving as a motion picture cameraman, I was assigned to General Patton's headquarters. We received word of the imminent linkup with an element of the Seventh United States Army coming up from Marseilles. There was more than one linkup, and they all came about the same time. I believe ours was a very interesting one—due to the personalities involved.

Locating the Second French Armored Division on the situation map, we left for their command post; there we were informed as to where and approximately when the meeting would take place. When we reached the town we headed for the railroad station, the designated meeting place. It was only a small town and this red brick building was easy to find. Three o'clock was the time the meeting was to take place, and every villager was at the station. Four o'clock passed, and with each passing minute one or two villagers would straggle away. Five o'clock came and the guard of honor which lined the street near the station was dismissed. With this gesture everyone but the photographers went to their homes. At five-fifteen, a jeep came speeding toward the station. It halted and on the bumper we saw "Seventh Army" and then the French tricolor, and we knew that they had arrived.

To our surprise a voice in perfect English said, "Is this the CP of the Second French Armored of the Third Army?" With this question, Eve Curie, a first lieutenant and liaison officer in the First French Armored, stepped from her jeep. Eve Curie, who returned from America to help her famed mother's adopted France, paid tribute to the two units in an informal talk and expressed hope for a speedy peace. With the liaison officer of the Second French Armored Division, the linkup took on an official air. We took some photographs, showing the Third and Seventh Army men together, and then the modest lady climbed back into her jeep and left for her unit. A machine gunner sat in the back seat behind his gun, as the road they had come over had not been traveled by Allied vehicles and small bands of Germans were roving the countryside. Completing our mission, we also returned to our headquarters, impressed by the gracious friendliness of Eve Curie.

—Technical Sergeant Warren Harding

Bridges over the Moselle, the 90th Infantry Division

THE RIVERS beyond Paris provided good photographic material, for in a river crossing, action and terrain are in an area limited enough to be entirely within the range of the camera—although natural and artificial atmospheric conditions are often adverse. Sgt. Warren Rothenberger tells of his experience at the Moselle River.

On November 5, 1944, the 90th Infantry Division, Third Army, to which my photo unit was attached, had as its objective to establish two bridgeheads across the Moselle River near the two small villages of Cattenom and Malling, France. The river itself was in bad shape, the Germans having blown several dams upstream and having flooded the countryside surrounding the vicinity of the prosposed bridge site.

On the night of the fourth, elements of one regiment were ferried across in assault boats, and after a bitter struggle they cleared the east side of the river to allow the engineers to start on the pontoon bridge. The next morning, three of us were at the Cattenom bridgehead site, shooting stills and movies. We were lending a very cool presence to an otherwise very hot spot.

The engineers had started early, and half a pontoon bridge was up by 8:00 A.M. when the Germans started throwing in a very accurate 88 barrage. With three direct hits they knocked the bridge out. It was then decided to throw the bridge over at night. Across the river the Germans held some high ground, making for some very accurate artillery and mortar fire. Obviously, these observation posts and mortar positions had to be knocked out. P47 fighter-bombers were called in to do the job using 500-pound fire-oil bombs. This meant good pictures, and we were in an excellent position to get them. We were on a slight hill behind a ridge that offered good cover from the damn mortars that were dropping uncomfortably close.

The planes came over and did a wonderful job. We worked like hell. I was shooting as fast as I could, although it was so cold I could hardly tear the tabs from my film pack. Twice the movie camera froze, causing much cursing and sweating. We got the pictures of the attack anyway.

The next day, the other three men of our unit went down again. The bridge wasn't up, and they took shots of the men and ammo being ferried across the river in assault boats. This had A-1 priority—ammo and food going over and the wounded and PWs coming back. Sergeant Tomko of our unit managed to bum a ride across and shot the infantry boys who were having a tough time of it on the east bank. All this time the weather was terrible—cold, rainy, and on top of it all water up to your knees wherever you went. (Bill Tomko received the Bronze Star. He learned via V-mail of the birth of his first child, Karen Ann, born October 19, 1944.)

For the next few days all of us worked hard. The Germans knocked the bridge out three times. We went twice to cover the Negro Chemical Smoke Generating Company that was doing a wonderful job of laying down a gigantic smoke screen. These men worked right out in the open on the river's edge and although the enemy artillery searched for them continuously, they kept right on grinding out the smoke.

Sometime around November 8 we went down to the Malling bridgehead site. They were still working on the bridge and assault boats were shuttling back and forth. I made movies here, mostly of PWs who, after being brought from the other side, were put to work as litter bearers, wading through the water. A lieutenant who was urging on the ammo bearers and PW litter bearers spied me and yelled, "What in the hell are you doing? We aren't supposed to use PWs for this sort of stuff and you can't make pictures of it!" I kept on shooting and finally he stopped yelling.

Stuff was coming in all of the time, mainly mortar shells, and every time we ducked we dipped our fannies in the water. We had a tough time keeping our cameras dry. All this time the weather was bad, and—plus the smoke screen—we had a lovely time with the exposures. Finally on November 11 the bridge was up, and early that morning two of us went down to film the actual crossing by infantry reinforcements and later artillery.

That was the Moselle crossing. We had shot about 2,400 feet of motion picture film and many still pictures. Later there were other river crossings, but I don't think any of them compared to that first Moselle crossing by the 90th Infantry Division.

—Sergeant Warren Rothenberger

Luxembourg, "Vive l'Américain!"

THE SMALL PRINCIPALITY of Luxembourg was like an opera setting: extremely clean and neatly kept cities and villages, with hospitable, well-dressed, self-respecting people. Modes and manners were more like home than those of France, and many soldiers found foster homes in Luxembourg. Sgt. John Blankenhorn relates the excitement of liberation.

During the first week in September, the 5th Armored Division proceeded from Sedan, up through a corner of Belgium, south of Arlens, and went about liberating southern Luxembourg (including Luxembourg City). Somewhere in the shuffle, the division had been joined by Prince Felix of Luxembourg (husband of the Grande Duchesse), who wished to be present when his country was liberated. The first vehicle of the division entered later. The prince came with the division's commanding general in a jeep, followed by me in a second jeep taking motion pictures of the prince's reception by the people. The reception was monumental; the people of Luxembourg are only slightly behind the French as handshakers and will break into tears of joy and sing the national anthem at the drop of a hat. Also, the Luxembourgers (both male and female) are, to say the least, artful at kissing GIs—which they do in crowd formation. So, the crowd stopped the prince's jeep, lifted him out onto several shoulders, and then everyone cried and sang.

I was also lifted out and took part of my movie coverage of the event supported by a clump of Luxembourgers. All this time the Germans had been sending in shells at odd intervals, and a common sight was to see a square jammed with people one minute and completely empty thirty seconds later. While these fantastic disappearing acts were taking place, the more militant patriots were having a field day. One happy character, for instance, had broken a show window in a huge department store and through it was taking Gestapo uniforms from a display and burning them on the sidewalk in front—all by himself, humming contentedly! The people were going berserk and roving around town. I never had fewer than fifteen passengers—all of whom were supposedly showing me the way someplace.

—Sergeant John Blankenhorn

47

Photography Diverted

UNDER the hazardous conditions of combat, soldiers begin to expect the unexpected. But Sgt. Paul Fox relates some humorous incidents that go beyond the normal routine of a combat photographer.

I was with the 5th Armored Division during the break-through to France. The 5th had knifed into Luxembourg, meeting light resistance. Outside the town of Nommern, we caught up with a Jerry convoy, cornered them in the town, and then gave them hell.

The main task force bypassed Nommern and left "Dog" Company of the light tanks to clean them out. I asked the tank commander if his force was going into the town right away. He said "Yes," so I started to walk into town by myself figuring that the tanks would be coming right in. I walked about four blocks before I reached the center of the village and still no tanks. There were a lot of civilians milling around the burning buildings; one woman was crying. She saw me with my movie camera which must have looked like a V weapon to her because when I started to take movies she shrieked twice as hard. Some of the braver townspeople timidly approached me and started to point toward the hills, evidently thinking I was German. I said, "No, no—I'm an *American* soldier." I no sooner said that than four or five people tried to kiss me at the same time! Then they asked me where the rest of the Americans were, and I said, "Oh, they'll be here any minute." Then I asked them where the Germans were, and they pointed toward the hills.

That's when the fun started. One of the families had some livestock in a burning building and since I represented the conquering American army, I was the logical one to get them out. Playing my role as expected, I brushed everyone aside, swaggered up to the barn door, and opened the door only to have a flame shoot out for about twenty-five feet. I lost interest in heroics fast.

The main road had cars parked all over, making it look like a used car lot. I started over to pick one out when a priest rushed out and said there were two Jerries behind his church. I put down my camera, drew my pistol, and advanced cautiously around the building. Suddenly a voice sang out in a British accent, "I say old boy, can you take us prisoners?" In the doorway stood two *Wehrmacht* (military machine) soldiers!

The tanks were still sitting outside the town. We had walked practically all the way back when we passed a cow whose leg had been shot off. The owner of the beast begged me to kill her, so I halted my prisoners and placed the pistol against the cow's head and fired. It didn't seem to have much effect—the cow just stood there. I put the pistol against her head again and fired. She still just stood there. But I didn't for long, as one of the light tanks opened up with a machine gun on us. All they saw were the prisoners. They heard gun shots and decided to fire back. After we picked ourselves off the ground, I turned around to see if the cow was still alive and there she was, apparently none the worse for her experience. I decided that was a job for a 75mm cannon and started to march the prisoners up to the tanks again.

When I arrived there the first thing I did was to ask who fired on me. They all looked a little uncomfortable, glanced at one another, and a PFC on one tank finally broke the awkward silence. He answered in a sheepish tone, "Aw, I was just kidding!"

—Sergeant Paul Fox

Impregnable Fort Driant Bypassed

WHEN the city of Metz fell, the forts in the mountains were so well constructed and defended that after a costly attempt to penetrate Fort Driant the remaining were bypassed and left to surrender. Sgt. R. H. Butterfield relates an experience at Fort Driant.

In October of 1944, Sgt. Russell Meyer, Pvt. Joe Lapine, and I drove up the narrow, muddy road through the forests on the hills in back of Metz. That was the only way to approach Fort Driant unobserved, for on the slopes and in the ravines artillery fired continuously. We were looking for an observation point from which we could see Fort Driant, one of the many major fortifications originally placed by the French and modernized by the Germans, which defended Metz from the hills.

At a command post we left the jeep and walked over the top of a ridge to an observation post under a tree. It was dug into the bank and protected on top by logs that had openings in front. From there we could look down upon the panorama of the Moselle River valley. Fort Verdun (on the top of the hill two miles across the valley) was visible, the slope around it pockmarked by scars of shell bursts. Upstream were two bridges across the Moselle, the target of artillery fire. White spouts of water in the stream showed the shell bursts. The city of Metz filled the valley farther upstream.

When Metz was captured the chain of forts that overlooked the city in the mountains continued to harass American communications. From these vantage points, the 5th commanded the city and roads on the plain westward, and the river valley, roads, and towns behind them. They were able to direct an accurate and troublesome artillery fire from stationary guns zeroed upon roads, intersections, bridges, and villages. Fort Driant was the control center of this fort system.

Fort Driant was concealed behind the perimeter of a ridge, a system of cement casements linked by connecting tunnels—all invisible from the valley below. The 5th Division spent a bitter, agonizing time fighting to get a few men past mines, booby traps, and cement into one of five casements. There they fought in the confines of tunnels where bazooka shells ricocheted down a corridor and explosions tumbled the roofs of compartments down upon both defenders and attackers.

On the crest of a ravine five hundred yards down the slope from the casement was a round, cement pillbox, the target for fire from one of our self-propelled guns located a hundred yards down to our right. While Sergeant Meyer from the observation post trained his camera on the pillbox, Private Lapine and I went to the SP gun. It was out on the edge of the woods on a road leading directly toward the tunnel, and as it fired a mission of eight rounds upon the pillbox we photographed them. The target was about five hundred yards away, so that both gun and target were visible in the range of the camera. It was a good scene photographically: the explosion of the gun, observers in the foreground, and dust spurting up as shells hit the earth. Some hit the battlement and caromed off the cement with no visible effect.

Then the turret of the pillbox slowly revolved toward us. We watched in fascination as the barrel pointed at us and fired. As the first shell of the self-propelled gun exploded in the trees we all took cover, running to dugouts. Shells burst in the trees above—limbs, branches, and shrapnel cracking and thumping down upon us. In a few minutes, when the barrage ended, the crew emerged from holes, cautiously at first, then hurriedly, and fired eight more rounds upon the target. We just as hurriedly returned to the observation post, where Sergeant Meyer had photographed the turret revolving toward him, the gun firing directly at the observation post, and the shells passing his position on the way to the SP gun.

The photography was an interesting sequence of proximity to enemy and American guns. Fort Driant was not taken but surrendered months later. In the casement that Americans had penetrated were pitiful remnants of their sacrifice: torn garments, discarded mess kits, and a helmet.

—Sergeant Ralph Butterfield

166th Signal Photo

A GI CROUCHES beside the protective cover of a tank and observes the smoke pouring from a tank recently hit by enemy fire.

166th Signal Pho

THE MOST FREQUENT FORM of advance by men in combat was to have a few GIs walk into inevitable enemy fire, sustain casualties, then overpower the Germans and advance to new positions.

THESE AMERICAN TANKS were destroyed in a frontal attack upon concrete casements at Fort Driant. The Germans kept the area denuded of vegetation and sown with mines.

Sgt. Ralph Butterfield

The 4th Armored Division Relieves Bastogne

WINTER in the Hurtgen Forest and the Schnee Eifel taxed the endurance of photographers as it did all troops whose duties included exposure to the elements. Besides the discomfort of numbed hands and feet was the effect of low temperatures, snow, and rain upon film and cameras. To this was added the emotional strain of sustained combat tension, built up in the liberation of France and now culminated in a temperamental and physical fatigue. Karl Von Rundstedt's counteroffensive in the Ardennes could not overrun besieged Bastogne, and at the "battered bastion" photographers performed their duties under inevitable emotional distress. Pvt. Sam Gilbert describes entering the town.

I was packing my equipment for a trip to photograph Mickey Rooney, who had just come into Third Corps with a special service company, when my photo officer called for me. "Gilbert," he said, "I've got a big story for you—even bigger than Mickey Rooney! The 101st Airborne is surrounded in Bastogne. The 4th Armored is on their way to relieve them. We want pictures." His voice grew loud and more determined. "We want action pictures—lots of smoke, fire, shells bursting in air, fire! Now Gilbert, let's show them what you can do. You go out there and get the pictures and don't forget to phone me the coverage report on time!"

The road to Bastogne was covered with snow—dry snow that swept the road in mystic whirlpools as our tanks and half-tracks pushed their way past the smoldering wreckage of our own lead vehicles. It snowed upon the grim procession of frightened youthful Jerry prisoners going one way, and cold, weary tankers going the opposite way. Upon this procession of Bastogne traffic looking down from the overhanging branches were shreds of human flesh and bits of charred OD (olive drab) clothing. And so it was that many who had helped open the road to Bastogne never knew of the glory and the military victory that they had helped achieve. Those still alive weren't thinking of glory. They were thinking of rest, of warmth, of home—of their job not yet done.

As we came closer to Bastogne the column came under heavy artillery bombardment. The driver and I left our jeep for cover along a ditch in the road. About five hundred yards off the road, I saw armored infantry working their way toward a woods where Jerries were really dug in. I sent the driver with the jeep to the next town in the rear, and told him I was going to try to get in with this infantry. During a letup in the barrage I ran across the field to join these doughboys. They would have been much happier to see me with a bazooka than with my Speed Graphic. Things were happening fast. They were moving up with marching fire, and that offered good picture possibilities.

I was kneeling, focusing on a rifleman about fifteen feet from me, when without realizing what had happened, I found myself knocked over backwards with snow and mud all over my camera, and the frantic cries of "Medic, Medic!" ringing in my ears. The rifleman whom I was photographing had been hit and a couple of other doughs right by me got shrapnel from that mortar. I got pictures of them being treated in a shell hole by a medic who worked calmly and joked with his patients as the Jerries let us have it. The boys were digging in so I worked my way back to the highway and asked an officer in the ditch how much farther I could go. He replied, "Son, this is as far as anyone has gone."

It was getting late so I hitchhiked back to the next town in hopes of getting my film into the message center. There I met a couple of civilian correspondents who were also trying to get into Bastogne, and we hopped into their jeep and started to go forward again. Everyone we asked told us we couldn't get into Bastogne—everyone but a lieutenant colonel who said, "Hell, yes—a couple of tanks just went in." We took another drink of cognac, pushed the accelerator to the floor, and didn't dare breathe until we were in Bastogne. Somehow we were lucky and made it!

In the town itself, there was no fighting when we arrived, only the aftermath of the arduous struggle: dead paratroopers lying in the town square and PWs under guard digging through the bombed rubble for bodies—bringing out the pieces of men and placing them in the silk supply parachutes which had been dropped. There were the paratroopers and the tankers each praising the other for what they had come through, and the town itself badly damaged from the fighting.

—Private Sam Gilbert

You are not all going to die. Only 2 percent of you in a major battle would die. Death must not be feared. Every man is frightened at first in battle. If he says he isn't he is a God damn liar.

—GENERAL GEORGE PATTON

Sgt. Arthur Herz

"THE ROAD TO BASTOGNE was covered with snow—dry snow that swept the road in mystic whirlpools as our tanks and half-tracks pushed their way past the smoldering wreckage of our own lead vehicles."

Sgt. Arthur He

GIs ON THE WAY to Bastogne. Small groups of American soldiers blunted the German attack in the Battle of the Bulge in the Ardennes. Under General Patton's command, elements of the Third Army made a well-executed pivot and fought northward to relieve Bastogne.

Sgt. Arthur Herz

WITHOUT white protective outer clothing and deprived of concealment by the snow, a patrol and machine gun cover were especially vulnerable to German fire.

THE RELIEF OF BASTOGNE, the first American tanks to penetrate through the Germans into the town, was a dramatic and tactically important event. For the companions of these GIs in the 4th Armored Division it was costly: 1,400 casualties along the snowy, windswept road.

Sgt. William Cumming

Requeim, Bastogne

EVERY PHOTOGRAPHER felt the voice of conscience at some time that winter—not so much personal as human. He felt it when he compared what he knew of death in the snow and mud with what was written about it beneath his photographs published in newspapers at home. Pvt. Donald Ornitz expressed what many have held unspoken.

There have been many articles about the 4th Armored Division's cut-through to relieve encircled Bastogne. Most appear written as if it were a ninety-yard run to score back in our football days at school. Remember that thrill, the fun and color then? This division's dash—actually our people stumbling over snow-covered ruts, bitter with exhaustion, cold, and hateful of everything—wasn't like that at all. We knew it then too; behind the headlines we felt the misery.

I remember Chaumont, a town two villages from Bastogne, equivalent to the crucial fifteen-yard line the day after the game. It was there I found my friends, their clothes blown off and shreds hanging on trees (I have photographs), their bodies dead—loss of blood; I could see the quantity, measurable on the snow.

These people did what they had to do well. And they were well led. I saw the maps—the care with which the facts were garnered. But now, the leaders, staff people before busy, conscientious with grease pencils, are proud, too proud. I'm not. My pictures were used, but not the ones I wanted seen—my friends dead. The job, telling what it cost in terms of people, I have hardly started. But how can the men who led be so proud? Their responsibilities as leaders, as survivors, to prevent more glorious military achievements haven't even begun. They are too busy having ribbons pinned on them for the dead's work and too busy observing the form of our close-order drill to see the dirty joke if it happens again.

—Private Donald Ornitz

HIS DECAPITATED BODY FROZEN with his arm extended, a German soldier gestures an ironic "Heil."

Sgt. William Ton

The German soldier in the Ardennes amazed his adversary. Short of transport, short of gasoline, short of artillery because of lack of transport and gasoline, his nation on the brink of defeat, he nevertheless fought with such courage and determination that the Americans saw him as fanatic.

—CHARLES B. MACDONALD, *A Time For Trumpets*

Visiting Firemen

HUMOR is never far from tragedy, and Cpl. Russell Grant found it on assignment in the Ardennes.

Following the Normandy breakthrough, our particular unit, which carried heavy newsreel equipment, was assigned to Patton's Third Army headquarters. Previously, as the Third Army was not as yet officially committed, we had done spot assignments on the local front. Though limited, these jobs were quite sufficient to convince me that the hero field was quite likely to be flooded; and anyway, as my mother didn't raise any stupid kids, I was more than content to live a simple, sheltered life, far removed from glory.

Later, an amazing variety of photo assignments came and went, most routine but some unusual. In one day I shot a wedding, a firing squad execution of German spies, and a visit by General Eisenhower. Most annoying were the visiting firemen, usually colonels and up, who flocked in from rear echelon units and pulled strings at army headquarters for permission to go sightseeing on active fronts under the guise of official business. They came flitting in from Paris, England, and even the United States, attracted by curiosity or the strange fascination that violence affords, and they usually demanded a photographer to go along and "record" evidence of enemy equipment or damage to our own armor. But I can visualize them in later years recounting tales of daring at the club or "snowing" their clamoring grandchildren and flashing my 4 × 5s as evidence.

I remember one occasion in midwinter when the Germans were holding stubbornly in northern Luxembourg, protecting their withdrawal from the Bulge. A major and full colonel blew in, waving papers and making much noise about inspecting U.S. artillery damage to the retreating enemy columns. As usual I drew the rear seat in a jeep, which is colder than a pawnbroker's eye at that time of the year. A few miles out, the party transferred to a half-track, where everybody had a seat—save me! With the track we got additions to the merry troupe, including a lieutenant from a 4th Armored unit, a gunner, and a captain and sergeant from a field artillery battalion.

The driver of the half-track had all the unpleasant attributes of a drunken New York taxi driver, and the vehicle skidded and careened along the narrow, snow-slushed roads through the snow-covered hills, bouncing the officers around like peas in a steel pod and interfering with their view of the bodies and wrecked vehicles along the way. We clattered past several batteries of 155s, one of which slyly waited until the track was in line of fire and cut loose, causing the colonel to slide gracefully off his seat and down the length of the bouncing vehicle on his official keister, where he came to rest sitting on my foot.

We passed through a small, burned-out town, and climbed a darkly wooded hill, where we pulled into an evergreen grove and halted. Two tanks and an armored car were edged into the woods along the road ahead and the tank men were gathered around a small fire. Occasional ambulances roared past, and across the clearing we could see a half dozen infantrymen poking disinterestedly along the fringe of the woods. The hilltop was a shambles: dead Jerries, horses, and over-turned wagons littered the shattered woods; bicycles, parts of bicycles, and parts of men hung from scrubby trees.

"Interdictory fire," explained the artillery captain. "We caught them yesterday morning; too bad it snowed last night as it covered up a lot of the mess." The group split up and the visiting firemen poked around, looking for helmets, and so forth—for souvenirs. I took photos of the colonel standing with one foot on a smashed Jerry ammo carrier along with several other shots. The major hustled over to get into some of the shots also, but the colonel remarked brusquely, "Let's get all those notes now, Major!" The Major never did get his "pitcher took." Intermittently, the air stirred with the long-drawn sigh of outgoing shells. The colonel glanced up as a flock went over and inquired whether there were many incoming ones. "Occasionally," said one of the armored boys. "They don't bother us much while the Cubs are up." He had hardly finished speaking when there was a nasty skittering whistle, and a sharp "Wham!" from the foot of the hill. "What the hell was that?" asked the major. "Guess they are still trying for the intersection down in the village," was the reply.

The major looked at the colonel and the colonel looked at the major. Then they both looked at their watches. Three more came; they didn't sound any better than the first. The eagle asked the gold leaf if he thought they had covered about everything around here, and did he think they should start back now? The major said it was up to the colonel, and as a matter of fact, it *was* getting a bit late! The tanker put an end to the buck-passing by informing no one in particular that the shells were hitting the area we had just come through on the way up here. He suggested we wait till the fire stopped, as "there wasn't much possibility of the bridge being cut anyway." He also said something about Jerry not having the observation we do, while the colonel and major regarded him with a gaze akin to outright distaste.

Half an hour later, we were grinding along the slope leading down to the town. It was nearly five o'clock—the half-light of early winter dusk was closing in. To the east, about eight P38s showed up and started a daisy chain, driving into the valley and machine-gunning something. We saw the tracers streaking down from their leading edges in the dives, but the sound didn't reach back until they had rocketed up from the dive and started to turn back. As each lightning went down, an enemy tracer boomed up briefly, like sparks from a burning chimney. Down in the town ahead, a building suddenly burned. The artillery captain leaned forward and shouted to the driver, "Keep her moving across this intersection!" The visiting major clenched his cigar tighter and stared straight ahead. The colonel echoed, "Yeah, keep her moving across the damn intersection."

—Corporal Russell Grant

ON A HILLSIDE above the Rhine River 89th Division GIs at a machine gun cover the impending river crossing site at Oberwesel. River crossings in France had resulted in severe casualties to American forces. The largest river to cross, the Rhine, was consequently approached with apprehension. With swift current and great width, it was an imposing obstacle. As the last barrier to the German heartland, rich in Germanic lore, it was assumed that the enemy resistance would be fanatic.

166th Signal Photo

Sgt. Arthur He

CROSSING PREPARATIONS included fog generators, visible behind the men, which spewed out protective clouds of obscuring mist that filled the river valley. Harassed by sporadic enemy fire, infantrymen of the 89th Division work their way along the riverfront at Oberwesel.

Crossing the Rhine

THE RHINE was approached and we consolidated the bank from Switzerland to the North Sea. The Allied armies were grouped in such force that once the Remagen bridge was seized and the east bank assured, the slow advance during winter was behind us. The sun dried muddy roads and shone on a profusion of surrender flags in German frame buildings, producing a white, checkered effect in the streets of small villages. Ground haze in the Rhine Valley was augmented by smoke from hundreds of generators that concealed the location of crossing intentions. Sergeant Caliendo took cover by a wall where a black soldier was faithfully tending his generator. When asked how much shelling was going on at the river a few blocks away, he replied, "I don't know what's doin' down there sergeant, but I'm makin' smoke!" Private Nesterach tells of his experience photographing a Rhine crossing.

As our forces reached the Rhine River at Nierstein, special types of naval craft and supplies cluttered the fields on the bank of the river for approximately five miles to our rear. At daybreak of the eventful day, the river was booming with activity. Men were building ferries and a pontoon bridge and hoisting landing craft, vehicles, and personnel boats into the river. Enough of a force was taken across to prepare ferry dockings—all was going smoothly, the enemy inactive. Perhaps to counteract possible losses from boat crossings, ten liaison planes, capable of carrying two men each, were readied at different fields along this front to land doughfeet on the east bank. At the proposed time of departure, flight orders were rescinded by the success of the boat crossing.

By 0800 hours, a full battalion of the 5th Infanty Division crossed the river in LCVPs (landing craft, vehicle, personnel), while ferries landed larger vehicles and one pontoon bridge was completed from the east to the west bank. After I photographed all the phases of the preparatory step and infantry came marching over to the river bank and loaded the LCVPs, by hopping on the same boat, I got scenes of them loading, embarking, crossing, and disembarking on the east bank of the Rhine. While on the east bank, after about a dozen boats had crossed, a Nazi fighter-bomber zoomed down, attempting with no success to shoot up the half-completed pontoon bridge. With the first blast of the plane's strafing guns, the riverbank's activity stilled, and all dove for cover. I chose the nearest foxhole cover, and as the plane zoomed overhead two butts protruded from it, mine and the owner of the foxhole who arrived in it the same time I did!

At about noon at another point on the river, amphibious tanks began crossing. Civilian spectators crowded the walled houses, peering through windows in amazement at our amphibious equipment. Two or three tanks had crossed when I arrived at the crossing, and just then another one rumbled down into the water, gurgled, and sank, resting on the river bottom. The tank crew, clothed in heavy combat clothes, scrambled over the side into the river. A motorboat crew of the Bridge Assemble Engineers' Battalion was on hand and pulled some of the crew into their boat. GIs on the shore tore off their clothing, dove into the river, and rescued two others. The entire crew was saved. The other tanks continued to cross, steering around the sunken tank.

The first day of the crossing was performed without the aid of a smoke screen and was a bright sunny day. As one pontoon bridge was completed, another was started and used for one-way traffic. Wounded and prisoners were returning on one, and on the other bridge, supplies, ammunition, and men were moving quickly across the Rhine into Germany.

—Private Nesterach

The quicker they are whipped, the quicker we go home. The shortest way home is through Berlin.

—GENERAL GEORGE PATTON

AMPHIBIOUS TANKS, their skirts folded and unused, rolled across the Rhine on the pontoon bridge at Boppard on March 26, 1945. The day before, amidst the trees on the hillside above the town, stubby fog generators filled the Rhine Valley with artificial smoke. In the obscuring mist army engineers of the 87th Division constructed the bridge.

Sgt. Ralph Butterfield

ON THE EAST BANK of the Rhine at Filsen, American forces, after crossing the river on a pontoon bridge, pause beneath picturesque vineyards and hotels in preparation for the drive into the heart of Germany.

Sgt. Ralph Butterfield

The German Autobahn

AMERICAN MEN, familiar from childhood with automobile travel, gave grudging admiration to the German superhighway, the Reichsautobahn. These are six-lane roads, constructed in the late 1930s, and are divided in the middle by a twenty-foot strip. We noticed the absence of advertising signs along the route, the beauty of the highway curving gracefully through the forest and valleys. We admired them and yet felt anger and disgust toward the people who turned such creative capacity into killing and destruction. Sgt. William Tomko, attached to one of Patton's armored divisions, was among the first to reach the Reichsautobahn.

It was in the early part of April that I got my first glimpse of Hitler's first major military project, the *Reichsautobahn*. I was with the 6th Armored Division, and we were spearheading toward the Rhine, when just outside Bad Dürkheim, our tanks were being sidetracked because of a destroyed bridge ahead. Near this huge pile of concrete rubble was a large sign—*EINFAHRT AUTOBAHN* (entrance to autobahn). This was my first contact with one of Hitler's twentieth-century wonders.

It was designed for the *Wehrmacht*. This was Hitler's dream—a spiderlike network of superhighways through the *Reich*, whereby Hitler could move whole armies, particularly his "elite" panzer divisions (armored), across Germany within twenty-four hours. And the Hitler plan was indeed "super," except of course it now was our Allied troops who could move with lightning speed. As Allied Aircraft methodically sought out and destroyed the German aircraft fields, Hitler was forced to use the autobahn for his latest weapon—the ME-262 Jet aircraft. We saw for the first time propellerless airplanes, totally unheard of at that time, strafing us and machine-gunning our troops as we sped along the autobahn. This was Hitler's last secret weapon, and thank God, they were too few, too late!

The U.S. 6th Armored Division rolled into Frankfurt, the first major city to be taken east of the Rhine. German resistance became disor-

ganized and thoroughly confused. Small American units were bringing in overwhelmingly large numbers of German prisoners. At some
points, the number of PWs were so great that a MP (military police)
would set up a prisoner compound single-handedly along the roadside.
At one of these compounds, I noticed three young soldiers, and upon
close inspection I was shocked to see that fourteen-year-olds had taken
up arms in the cause for Hitler. What a pathetic sight, as I lined up the
three youths for a picture!

—Sergeant William Tomko

---

*"I WAS SHOCKED to see fourteen-year-olds had taken up arms in the
cause for Hitler."*

Sgt. William Tomko

Nuremberg, Nazi Shrine

IN THE COUNTRY it was orderly. The cities were de-
stroyed—acres of heaped stone, twisted iron, gutted build-
ings: Prum, Koblenz, Karlsruhe, Frankfurt, Plauen, Nurem-
berg, Munich, Mainz, and Mannheim. Their individuality
was gone, reduced to a common destruction. Cpl. Harry Mil-
ler entered Nuremberg when it was taken. ‗

The 80th Division, after taking Bamberg, teamed up with the 45th Division to encircle Nuremberg, the city used by the Nazi party for its yearly gatherings and meetings. Under the leadership of Julius Streicher, dictator of the Nuremberg Laws, several thousand *Volkstrum* troops defended the city.

The fighting was heavy for four days and nights; it was a house-to-house, street-to-street battle. As the 80th advanced farther into the city, it became apparent that Julius Streicher had led his troops into mass suicide, as the streets were littered with dead Germans. The advance passed where on March 30, 1933, the giant book burning took place. Here the books that did not meet with the approval of the Nazi teachings were destroyed. It was a strange coincidence that exactly twelve years later the 80th Division won that section of Nuremberg.

Still, more than half of Nuremberg had to be taken. The division advance passed the Brown House, in which all the Nazi atrocity laws were made under the leadership of Streicher, and then to the famous Leopold Arena and Nuremberg Stadium, where for many years the annual Nazi meetings were held. A few Nazi *Volkstrum* troops who had survived raised the flags of surrender, and the city was completely taken over by the 80th Division.

Nuremberg is divided into two parts known as the new and old Nuremberg. In the old Nuremberg, there are several underground tunnels built during the fifteenth century—in some sections five levels below the surface. Together with my combat pictures of the fighting, the photos of the tunnels made my coverage of Nuremberg complete. After the fighting ceased, I met Sgt. Fred Selling of New York City with the 80th Division, who was born in Nuremberg and who knew the tunneled city very well. We decided to investigate the tunnels and found that not only had the Nazi party rebuilt them into modern underground offices but also that many Nazi officials had committed suicide there and lay dead!

—Corporal Harry Miller

Surrender Negotiations

EVERY SOLDIER who participated in the war has personal, human anecdotes that they have told since the war. The following tells how Sergeant Caliendo and Corporal Herz not only found good photography in the city renowned for Luther's and Goethe's houses but unexpected adventure as well.

The name of the town was Eisenach. It was isolated and almost completely surrounded by troops of the 89th Infantry Division. Time was precious and to avoid unnecessary casualties the commanding general, General Finkley, decided to try to initiate a surrender. Consequently a major on the staff of General Finkley, accompanied by combat cameraman Sgt. Barney Caliendo of Los Angeles and Cpl. Arthur Herz of Rochester—both of the 166th Signal Photo Company—drove into Eisenach flying the white flag of truce.

The first German soldier encountered on the road was asked to take the American party to the *Wehrmacht* headquarters. The fellow was somewhat confused; he did not blindfold anybody and permitted the Americans to note and evaluate the disposition and size of German defense in the streets. Once the Nazi headquarters had been reached, Herz and Caliendo jumped out of the jeep, shooting pictures of the headquarters building and the guards and officers who were standing about in confused bewilderment. This state of affairs did not last long, however. Three or four shouting Nazis rushed Herz trying to take his camera away, while Caliendo with grins meant to be reassuring to the Germans repeated "Alles ist Okay" and managed to keep the crowding Nazi soldiers from his camera. The two photographers, still doggedly hanging onto their cameras, finally made it to the conference room where the surrender negotiations took place.

Despite the major's repeated warning that at 1900 hours Eisenach would be subject to terrific artillery bombardment unless surrendered, the Nazi commanding general wanted to fight it out. It was 1840—twenty minutes before the scheduled bombardment—when the negotiations broke down with finality. Weapons were returned to the American party and this time they were blindfolded preparatory to being driven back to their own lines.

Yet there was one more most disconcerting delay. The Nazis decided to take away the signal corps photographers' film and cameras. Thus the two cameramen found themselves again being rushed by grabby SS characters who could not be put off, so following a fast pig latin discussion between the two cameramen, Caliendo offered to destroy the film in front of the Jerries if they would not bother with the cameras. While in the conference room, however, the photographers had reloaded their cameras which now held only unexposed film!

It was 1850—ten minutes to go—and everyone in the American party was getting nervous when the Germans agreed to the suggestion. So the two men opened their cameras, unraveling the unexposed film before the narrow scrutiny of the Jerries. The trick worked!

It was 1858 when the Americans finally crossed back into their lines, clearing by two minutes the doomed city, which then received four thousand rounds of artillery. Sergeant Caliendo and Corporal Herz brought with them motion picture and still shots showing German headquarters with mounted guards and other Nazi personnel. Also photographed were several bridges that were being prepared for demolition. For this piece of work in which they pulled the wool over the Jerries eyes, the two combat cameramen were commended by General Finkley.

—Sergeant Barney Caliendo and Corporal Arthur Herz

Candidly, General Patton

THE COLORFUL SPEECH and aggressive character of General Patton were well known to every Third Army soldier. Here Corporal Grant relates some instances.

For the last six months of the European war, I was assigned to cover General Patton's personal photographic needs at Third Army headquarters. The general was a camera fiend himself, possessing a Contax miniature which he used frequently with excellent results. At the Buchenwald Concentration Camp, near Weimar, Germany, I did a series for the War Crimes Commission. The general also had covered the camp with his Contax; later he called me into his office and informed me that he had seen my stuff and that he thought his photos were every bit as good as mine. I said, "Yes, SIR."

At Regensburg, on the Danube, Patton was visited by Bishop Henry Knox Sherrill of Massachusetts. The bishop rendered the V-E Day sermon at Third Army headquarters, which General Patton attended. The general listened intently, bowed his head and prayed, and sang all the hymns. I hurried out the door to catch a shot of the bishop and general together. When I finally got them posed, the general shattered the holy atmosphere by remarking to me, "Now for Crissake, don't squat down! Take the shot standing up!" He turned to the startled bishop and explained, "All these goddamn people insist on getting down on their knees to take their goddamn pictures."

On another occasion I rode behind the general to the 5th Infantry Division to cover the award of the Congressional Medal to one of their medics. He hung the ribbon on the boy's neck with the admonition, "Now don't go and get your ass shot off, after all this."

On the way back, as was his custom, Patton stopped and "chewed" no less than four different people for various infractions of regulations. The last stop was for two infantrymen who were chatting merrily with two girls. His driver brought the four-starred jeep to a screeching stop. The general stood up with his hands on the windshield and yelled, "Come here!" The two doughs were so scared they were rooted to the spot.

"Goddamn it," yelled Patton in his high-pitched voice, "Come here when I call you!" They rushed over, saluted, and stood shakily at attention. "What do you mean talking to those civilians?" he thundered, his face taking on the color of an Arizona sunset. The ranking GI croaked out that the girls were Russian refugees. Somewhat nonplussed, the general hesitated, then shouted, "Well get them the hell out of sight. Take them behind a hedge or something. . . . Drive on!"

—Corporal Russell Grant

GENERAL GEORGE S. PATTON JR., typically energetic, and General Eisenhower. General Patton was a complex man of astute military competency, religious faith with participation in church services, effective vocal vulgarity, dynamic personal leadership, and decisive command decision. He was regarded with both dislike and respect by most GIs.

The Prized Luger

CPL. CHARLES SUMNERS was as diligent as every solider is in the prize sought after by all: a Luger pistol. He got his surprisingly, and unexpectedly.

It occurred just outside the little town of Labits, located approximately twenty miles south of Leipzig. After cutting for the Leipzig-Chemnitz Autobahn, a task force of the 69th Tank Battalion, the 4th Armored Division Battalion, and the 44th Armored Infantry Battalion caught a company of German infantry retreating toward Leipzig. The Germans made no attempt to surrender and the GIs had no alternative other than to cut them down.

We halted our jeep near two fallen German soldiers, both quite obviously dead. One had been hit in the head with a 50-caliber round, the other bore no visible wound. My fellow photographer, Sgt. Russell Meyer of San Leandro, California, and I took several shots of the tanks and half-tracks passing by with the dead Germans in the foreground. Suddenly I thought I saw one of the figures move. I called Meyer's attention to it and went over to investigate. Insasmuch as Meyer could speak a little German, we hit upon a plan. Quite audibly I drew and cocked my .45 pistol. Then Meyer said in German, "This first soldier is not dead, come here and shoot him in the head." That did the trick. The apparently dead German jumped to his feet, begging for his life and yelling "Kamerad!" Net proceeds—one Nazi PW and one Luger pistol.

—Corporal Charles Sumners

Atrocities, a Prelude

GERMANY was beautiful. The fields were well cultivated, with vast tracts of forest and picturesque towns. Inconceivably brutal and ugly in the scene was the uncovered infamy of Nazi degradation—the concentration murder camps. Equally astonishing were the feelings of the civilians, who disclaimed any knowledge of, responsibility for, or curiosity about camps so close to them that they complained to the guards about the odor of the dead. The German people walked to work, and rode to church, by excavated and covered pits—the common burial grounds of thousands of their fellowmen who died from starvation and pestilence. They were angry, affronted, and hurt that they should be made to witness, apprehend, and dispose of the thousands of bodies in the barracks, on the ground, and in burial pits. Sergeant Cummings tells about the first one found—the one at Ohrdruff.

We were within one mile of the concentration laager and under constant shelling, with the CCB (combat control base) of the 4th Armored Division, when someone mentioned the Jerries were probably so ashamed of their work they were trying all the harder to keep the Americans away from their camp.

The first thing I noticed on reaching the camp was the odor; they had used lots of lime, but unless a body is buried within a week it takes more than lime to preserve it. The first sight that greeted me was forty men sprawled in death. They had been murderously machine-gunned as they waited for marching orders. I noticed one body on a stretcher and wondered why this one in particular had flowers. It seemed he had been an English flier, and the few girls of the camp had come and placed them there.

The next sight was the storeroom—bodies stacked up like cordwood. Days later, when the civilians were forced to look upon this spectacle of horror, some were violently sick.

The pit on the hill above the town where three thousand nationals were buried had a three-inch layer of reddish colored water. Blood—

from the dead of many countries mixed with mud—was in the coloring. One decayed leg was sticking out from a partially exhumed man. The pit was twenty yards long and ten wide. Bodies had been buried and stacked in layers. Beside the pit was a pyre of bodies. Our advance had interrupted ghoulish work. They were burning the bodies in layers of four on a grill—a grill of railroad rails. Torsos were blackened chunks. They had burned sixteen hundred bodies in two weeks; "they" were Nazi guards who sat on the edge of the pit and amused themselves by firing their rifles close to the Poles and Russians forced to exhume and burn their own countrymen.

This was Ohrdruff Concentration Laager.

—Sergeant William Cummings

"THE FIRST SIGHT that greeted me was forty men sprawled in death. They had been murderously machine-gunned as they waited for marching orders."

Sgt. Ralph Butterfie

Sgt. Ralph Butterfield

"BESIDE THE PIT was a pyre of bodies. Our advance had inter-
rupted ghoulish work. They were burning the bodies in layers of four
on a grill—a grill of railroad rails."

A GERMAN CIVILIAN from the town of Ohrdruff appeared at the nearby concentration laager and authoritatively acted as a self-appointed guide, showing the American soldiers the horrors of the camp. About a dozen inmate survivors of the camp became very angry. They excitedly endeavored to make the Americans understand that the German was not only a guard at the camp but also unsually cruel. Failing to communicate, as none spoke English, they acted.

Sgt. Ralph Butterfield

SEIZING STOOLS AND TABLES from a nearby barracks they suddenly and ferociously attacked the German. Before the soldiers could intervene, he was beaten to death.

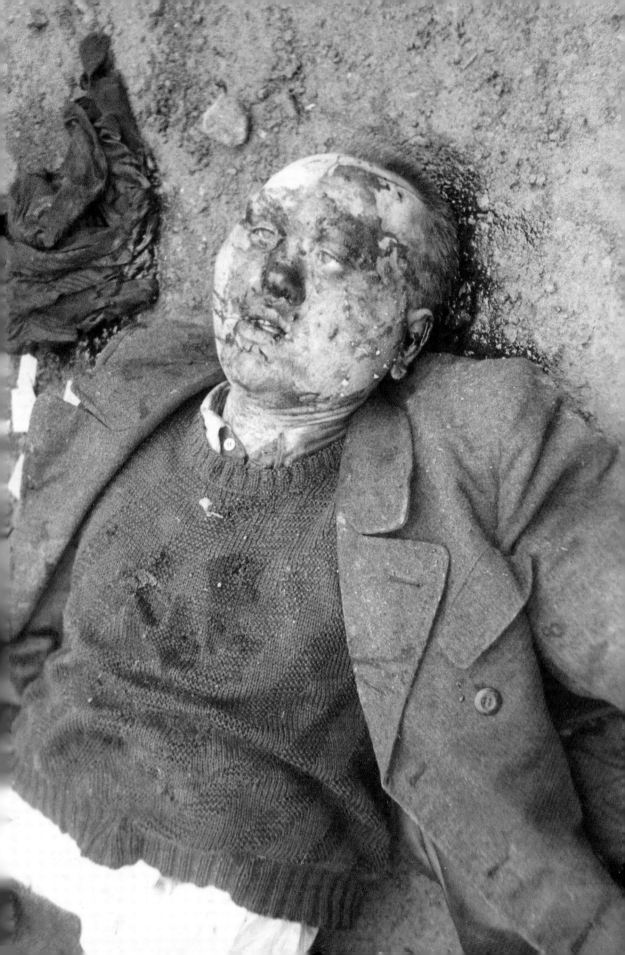

Holocaust Photography

THE GUILT of the German people, it was decided, would be determined by evidence against individuals and groups. Pvt. Louis Dougall worked on gathering photographic data.

I n addition to the regular and routine experiences of following the battle from the beaches to the Czech and Austrian borders, Sgt. Robert Sawyer, New York City, and I were withdrawn from our regular assignments to work with the Third Army headquarter's Judge Advocate Section, investigating German war crimes and atrocities committed in the Third Army area. They equipped us fully, gave us an official sounding paper that would open the Bank of England, pointed to a spot on the map, and told us to go to it.

We covered a lot of ground and saw many direction signs in our visits to such camps as Buchenwald, Mauthausen, Flessenberg, Dachau, and the little-heard-of crimes—which were nonetheless horrible—in such cities as Wetterfield, Amberg, Nuremberg, and Bayreuth. To say the least, our job was a stinking one. Many times we had to have bodies of men and women long dead dug up to investigate the killings of slave labor personnel in forested areas, because the SS and fanatical Nazis marched these walking skeletons from camp to camp, away from the encroaching front lines.

It was satisfying to learn that the Judge Advocate Section had a lot of information and evidence against the German people responsible for the crime and injustice at these camps and that much was being done to prosecute them. Wherever possible, we arranged to have the crimes brought to the attention of the local populace. The case at Nuremberg was ideal and done up in detail.

About one hundred and sixty slave labor men had been killed and buried in three shallow pits in a pine tree grove approximately two miles from the town of Nuremberg, Germany. Arrangements were made to have them dug up and have individual coffins made for the murdered men, who were being laid out on the wooded hillside. Everything had to be ready for Sunday morning. Meanwhile it had rained, washing off the dirt and sand from the bodies and making things more effective for the scheduled program.

Appropriately enough, Sunday was a brisk, sunshiny day, and the townspeople, as ordered, turned out en masse and lined both sides of the main street. At the appointed hour, and with cameras already placed at strategic points to record each step of the proceedings, four men of the town stepped forward, grasped a coffin, and began the two-mile trek to the scene of the crime. Eventually there were no men left to carry the bodies, and the women and girls of the town were enlisted to make the trip to the grave, secure a body, place it in the crudely made coffin, and again with a person at each corner of the coffin, make the trip back to town through the lined streets, and then to the Nuremberg cemetery where a ceremony would be held.

Several of the men and women quailed at the proceedings, fainted away, or otherwise would have quit, but the program was kept moving. It was a strange and ghastly sight to see a two-mile-long procession of groups of five people—one of them in an uncovered coffin, dead of an unjust and horrible death, the other four trailing in file through the town to the cemetery.

There, among the tombstones of the townspeople's dead, the bodies were laid side by side. Everyone—men, women, and children alike—was made to attend commemorative services held by several army chaplains and a rabbi who had known many of the dead who lay before him. After this was all over, every adult and child was made to walk singly by the rows of rain-washed bodies that lined the walks of the cemetery in the open coffins, and each was made to see the irrefutable evidence of crimes committed by the regime they supported.

The final phase of the ceremony was the placement of lids on the coffins and interment of the bodies in a large, separate grave apart from those of the Germans. Because very few men could be identified, no separate markers were erected; however, a permanent stone monument to these men, telling of the brutal way in which they died, was erected and will be maintained in the small town of Nuremberg, Germany.

—Private Louis Dougall

FROM France, Italy, Poland, Holland, Belgium, Scandinavia, and other countries, thousands of men and women were transported to Germany and forced to labor on farms and in factories. Released from captivity near Prum by the American forces, these men organized themselves into a march toward Poland.

Sgt. Ralph Butterfield

Sgt. Ralph Butterf.

ON A SNOWY AFTERNOON Hungarian soldiers formed a funeral procession for several of their compatriots who were killed when their camp at Moosburg, Germany, was liberated.

HITLER COMMENCED his vision of German destiny by occupying the Sudetenland in 1938 through the Munich Pact. Restored to Czechoslovakia in 1945, the German-speaking occupants were expelled. Many families loaded their possessions upon carts and, in long processions, made the trek to adjacent Germany.

Sgt. Ralph Butterfield

American Prisoners of War

OTHER CAMPS—especially Allied prisoner-of-war enclo-sures—were anticipated and sought after by American forces. There were many, large and small, and the Third Army liberated a great number of them in southern Ger-many. Many of the prisoners had been in several PW camps, traveling on foot hundreds of miles, often under harsh climatic conditions in which exposure too often proved fatal. Cpl. Billy A. Newhouse, however, had the happy coincidence of meeting hometown friends in one camp.

By the time the Allied troops crossed the Rhine River, it was evident that Germany had been defeated and the remaining action would be one of mopping up the routed enemy troops. So far as combat photography was concerned, every phase had been completely covered and any additional coverage would only be repetitious, except for certain spe-cific engagements. Orders came down to be on the lookout for subjects of interest that could not be photographed outside Germany proper. Among these subjects were the concentration and prisoner-of-war camps.

As we pushed eastward from the Rhine we ran into PW camps, but in each there were only a handful of Americans present—the bulk of British and American troops having been moved into the heart of Ger-many. The first PW camp we had the opportunity to photograph was in Limburg, Germany. By the time we reached there, it had been cleaned up considerably and we were not able to make a photographic record of it as it was before liberation. We were, however, given very vivid descriptions by our guide, a paratrooper of the British Red Devils who had been captured during the ill-fated operation at Arnhem, Holland. The largest compound was French, then the Russian, British, Indian, Italian, and the smallest was the American group—numbering one hundred and fifty.

Living conditions for the French were comparatively good. They received adequate medical supplies and were issued Red Cross parcels regularly. Their barracks were crowded, but each man had a wooden bunk. The remainder of the camp was forced to live in miserable conditions. Men slept on filthy straw on the floors with overcoats or burlap bags for coverings. Sanitary facilities were practically nonexistent and dysentery spread like fire.

The German food ration consisted of a bowl of thin mush served at 6:00 A.M. and a bowl of watery soup served at 7:00 P.M. Each man received one kilogram of bread per day, and once a week boiled potatoes and ten grams of meat. Red Cross parcels were issued irregularly to the Americans and British, with the excuse that with the disruption of rail transportation the packages could not be delivered at regular intervals.

As we drove farther into Germany, I was excited to come across a camp in which there was a large number of American prisoners because several of my friends in the air force, who had been shot down over enemy territory, had been reported as prisoners of war. Two weeks before V-E Day, while our unit was attached to the 14th Armored Division, the PW camp at Moosburg, Germany, was liberated, freeing seventy thousand American, British, Italian, and Russian prisoners.

The camp had been freed at 10:00 A.M. and when we drove in at 6:00 P.M., the inmates were not used to the fact that they were free. We made a mistake by driving our jeep into the compound. Picture taking was an impossibility because we were immediately surrounded by thousands of Americans, each anxious to know how the war was progressing, where his unit was located, how long it would be before they got food, and when they could be evacuated. The sight of the jeep brought some of the men almost to the point of tears. They closed in around it staring blankly at it, and those who were close reached out to touch it—just to be touching something that was American. Someone yelled "Blow the horn," and then it started. Men took turns sitting in or on the jeep and blowing the horn until we were ready to leave.

I climbed to the top of a fence post to take a shot of the assembled group. After tripping the shutter I heard a voice say, "What the hell are you doing up there?" I looked down and at the foot of the pole I spotted Capt. Chester Pasternak, CO of the 2nd Battalion, 314th Regiment, 79th Division, with whom we had worked several times while we were attached to the 79th Division. I climbed down and talked with him a few minutes about the activities of his outfit after we left the division, how he was captured, how long he had been in, and so forth. A thought struck me, and making a stab in the dark I asked if anyone knew Lt. Vincent Shank or Lt. L. Bascom, two fellows with whom I had gone to high school and who I knew were in the same camp together somewhere in Germany. A fellow standing at my elbow spoke up, "I know them both. Come on and I'll show you where they are!"

The two fellows informed me that a third Corona, California, man was also in the camp, Lt. James Pirtle. We invited the three to spend the night with us and we had no trouble inducing them to come. As we drove back to our location, we passed a large group of German prisoners, including some of the guards and the commandant of the camp. Lieutenant Shank remarked on seeing them, "It just doesn't seem possible that this morning we were prisoners, and this evening we are free and they are prisoners!''

For chow that evening we had all the fresh eggs we could eat, "liberated" from a nearby farm. While we waited for the eggs to be cooked, the three fellows spent the time eating bread and jam. After downing three slices apiece it dawned on them that they were stuffing themselves and would not be able to eat the eggs. The temptation of real food was too great and each ate another piece of bread. But this didn't stop them from eating fourteen eggs apiece!

We were naturally interested to learn of conditions in the camp and to hear some of their experiences. Lieutenant Shank and Lieutenant Bascom had both been held for twenty-two months and Lieutenant Pirtle for six. Lack of food and fuel were the greatest discomforts these men had suffered. They each said they would have starved had it not been for the Red Cross parcels they received. The food the Germans gave them was not enough to keep a man alive nor was it fit to eat. For fuel they had torn out the panels separating the toilets in the latrine and ripped up the floors in the barracks.

A good many of the officers in the camp at Moosburg were forced to march from a camp south of Berlin to Moosburg in February. They were a little more fortunate than some prisoners who were marched to new locations in that their guards averaged from forty-five to fifty-five years old. The guards marched them slowly because of their own age and found barns for them to sleep in at night.

From the chance meeting of my friends, by visiting other camps, and by talking to men who spent time in German PW camps, we came to the conclusion that prison conditions at their best were far from good. There were no standard conditions maintained, and conditions depended upon the individual personnel of the various camps.

—Corporal Billy A. Newhouse

Sgt. Ralph Butterfield

WITH BITTER RAGE and ghoulish ferocity this poster, entitled Hitler, Lover of Mankind, *announced an exhibit of atrocity photographs in Prague in 1945. The whispered rumors in Eastern Europe about the so-called labor camps became monstrous reality when the concentration camps were liberated.*

Cpl. Billy A. Newhouse

"I CLIMBED to the top of a fence post to take a shot of the assembled group."

Deliverance

AFTER SUFFERING under nearly unbearable hardships in the concentration camps, it took many of the PWs time to adjust to the reality of their new freedom once their camp had been liberated. Sergeant Butterfield describes the effect that a visit from General Patton had on the newly freed prisoners at Moosburg, Germany.

At Moosburg a distinguishing coloration of dull, gray-brown and green tones was pervasive, as in most prisoner-of-war and concentration camps. The wooden frame buildings were covered with grayish tar paper. The interiors were unpainted, darkened, bare wood—grimy and soiled. The inmates' clothing became faded and creased, wrinkled and patched. In frequent poor weather, dull gray clouds hovered over the buildings and dirt grounds like a pall. The faces of the men were pallid from lack of sunlight and undernourishment.

On the day of liberation the excited prisoners roamed the encampment from one event to another. A loud shriek of a siren from a vehicle at the gate drew their interest, and they walked and ran toward the entrance with excited anticipation, crowding around it in a mass of hundreds of men. The excited conversation of those at the gate became hushed, and those in the rear could see that the men were parting to make way for someone who had entered the gate and was walking through their midst. The passageway was wide, fully forty feet, and the sight was immediately quieting.

Gold stars gleamed upon his helmet liner, which was lacquered to lustrous brightness—a gleaming orb. His jacket was rich maroon, with flecks of the bright color of the decorations on his chest. At his belt the two ivory-handled revolvers glistened, and his fawn-colored riding pants were tucked into highly polished riding boots. The contrast to the pallidness of the camp coloration was astonishing, dramatic, and emotional.

General Patton looked neither right nor left as he marched rapidly, purposefully, down the middle of the avenue. His presence was larger than life, a stature these men had been deprived of for months. Hundreds of eyes followed his progress with incredulous, enrapt concentration. The silence was like a void, not a sound save for the rap of his boot heels, no movement of hand or foot—the silence of men deeply moved. He marched within the camp, his helmet gleaming above the hundreds of men who parted their ranks in front of him. There was no personal, familiar rapport, but instead a remote, powerful imprint of his commanding presence.

A major standing in front of me, his uniform slack and wrinkled, turned aside when Patton had passed and in a reflective voice, to no one in particular, remarked, "Well, I have seen Jesus Christ himself, now." He spoke in a declarative tone, neither reverently nor irreverently, but rather with acknowledgment that Patton had verified his deliverance.

—Sergeant Ralph Butterfield

Nazdar, President Benes

V-E DAY came and passed, and celebration among the troops was conspicuous by its moderation. For the most part the war did not end as much as die, and death is sobering, not demonstrative. Photographic work continued at a strong pace: mass surrenders, murder camps, and displaced persons. American forces liberated the western portion of Czechoslovakia, a country with great democratic vitality. A motion picture sound unit went from Pilsen to the capital city of Prague and filmed the return and celebration procession of President Benes to his country. Sgt. Harry Downard related the unique experience.

The day following the taking of Prague by the Russians, Sergeant Harding, Sergeant Butterfield, and I, a three-man photo team, were on our way to Prague with our motion picture sound camera. Upon arriving at the demarcation line separating the American and Russian territories, we were stopped by Russian guards, whose orders were to allow no American soldiers to enter the Russian territory. By a long process of signs with our hands and saying over and over "General Eisenhower, General Patton, and President Benes photo" we finally convinced them to allow us to pass on to Prague. We were given authority by a few sentences written on a small piece of notepaper by a Russian officer.

The roads were jammed with Russian vehicles consisting of the American three-quarter-ton trucks and the two-and-one-half-ton trucks mixed with the Russian horse-drawn wagons. The Russian soldiers, upon seeing that we were Americans, would shout "Komerad," running up to us and giving us such bear hugs that we could hardly breathe. Of course we exchanged American cigarettes for Russian ones, and there was a wonderful feeling of comradeship and festivity in the air.

We were among the first Americans to arrive in Prague and were more than warmly welcomed by the civilians. No matter where we parked our truck, it was immediately surrounded by civilians who wished to shake our hands. Many of the people could speak English and were very eager to converse with us, as it was their first opportunity to speak English in six years. During the German occupation it was forbidden to speak our tongue.

The Czechs were more like Americans than any people we had met in Europe. They had a great regard for America and knew all our film stars and our modern music prior to the last six years. Many of the people had relatives or friends living in America and spoke longingly of coming to our country.

We were in Prague at the time President Benes returned from six years in exile. Despite a certain amount of difficulty with the Russian woman military police, who directed traffic with a grand flourish of flags, we were able to gain a position in the parade near the president. The streets were lined with women dressed in their colorful native costumes, cheering as the president passed in review. There were many Russian cameramen taking pictures also, and we carried one with us to help get through several traffic blocks.

The parade of motor cars started at the Woodrow Wilson Railroad Station and proceeded rapidly along several miles of city streets. Thousands of people filled the sidewalks and waved from buildings, shouting "Nazdar!"—the Czech salutation. The parade ended at Prague Old Town Square, where President Benes addressed several hundred thousand people who had assembled there.

In the late afternoon of the same day we were granted a personal interview with the president. We crossed the Charles Bridge and ascended the hill to the Hradcany Castle, a magnificent, enormous edifice overlooking the river and city. In his private chamber the president gave us an address in English for our sound camera. Afterwards we talked for twenty minutes about conditions in America and Germany. He mentioned Colonel Lindbergh being in the same room we were in. "He stood where you are standing." He mentioned the disbelief in America in 1937 about German military intentions and his own happiness that Czechoslovakia was free.

We were all very much thrilled by our good fortune in meeting the president, especially since we were the only Allied cameramen who were able to get through the Russian lines and film this important event.

Sgt. Ralph Butterfield

HUNDREDS OF WOMEN celebrated the return of President Benes to Prague in 1945 by wearing the Czech national costume. With bright red and green designs upon white skirts, elaborate lace decorations, and headpieces of flowers and buds, they were a colorful contrast to the urban streets.

Later I returned to Prague several times, photographing such activities as the return of Allied prisoners, the arrival of the American Legation, and the arrival of UNNRA (United Nations NATO Refugee Association) food and supplies. During the last trip we were detained by the Russian military police, who confiscated our pass and expelled us from the city.

My visits to Prague will always remain in my memory as the most pleasant and enjoyable of my war years in Europe.

—Sergeant Harry Downard

II

RECOLLECTIONS years after the war, while immersed in civilian life and deprived of spontaneity, benefited from the assimilation of wartime experiences. Many events became indelibly imprinted within memory. The following episodes were recalled in the years after the war.

Viewfinders

OCCASIONALLY photographers became involved in military actions remote from their normal duties. In the following events, Sgt. Barney Caliendo and Lt. Adrien Salvas combined photographic opportunities with unusual combat participation.

We were driving along the Moselle, Lieutenant Salvas and I, and we could not find a thing to photograph—no action at all, not a GI anywhere. It was one o'clock in the afternoon, and finally we spotted a jeep with artillery on the bumper. We stopped, identified ourselves as photographers, and asked the colonel if there was any action of interest. "Yes," he replied, "at about four o'clock the infantry is going to cross the river. Last night we set up a forward observation post for the artillery." We said that would be great, and could he show it to us. He replied, "I can't really show it to you, but I can show you how to get to it. Follow me, but don't raise any dust; we'll draw fire."

We followed him along a dirt road and stopped at the edge of a forest. We got out, went over to him, and he said, "Okay, this is as far as the jeeps go. You see that wire? Follow it through the trees to the next opening. When you go across it, crouch; we don't want Germans to see any activity going on."

So we followed the wire and crouched down as we crossed the open space and got to the edge of the forest. I heard artillery coming in. It came in very fast. I thought it was ours. I hit the ground, and so did Lieutenant Salvas. But it was not our stuff going out; it was theirs, and it hit the forest ahead of us. It was not close to us. When it stopped we followed the wire and came to a hole where the artillery observers were. Apparently the shell had hit them. They were both dead.

However, they had been there long enough to set up their tripod with a scope and their maps with the telephone. We did not know what to do. We looked through the scope viewfinder, and by George, in the forest across the river, we could see two machine gun nests. Lieutenant Salvas picked up the phone and identified himself. He said, "We are two men up here, two photographers, and your two men are dead here. We looked through the scope, and we see machine gun nests." The rear told us, "Look at the map, and give us as close a coordinate as you can." We were not map readers, and we were looking into a forest

101

across the river. There were no roads to identify, nothing to relate to a position on the map. Lieutenant Salvas and I guessed and gave them a coordinate.

They replied that they would shoot one round, then we would tell them how far off they were. We could hear the gun fire and hear the round come overhead and burst. It was about two hundred yards over and about one hundred yards left of the target. We told them of the location, and they said, "That is good enough for us. We will send in six rounds."

In the meantime I had put the twenty-inch lens and the viewfinder on the camera. I set that on the portable tripod, and focused in on the nests. The six rounds came in and tore up the forest. I had the camera going all the time. We looked into the scope after the smoke cleared. We could see some activity of the Germans shoveling dirt. We phoned that they were very close, and why not send in six more? They agreed. Six more hit the location, and we saw no more motion.

We sat there. They told us, "At four o'clock the infantry was going to cross the Moselle. At about a quarter to four we are going to start a barrage on the hill. Stay there." We stayed.

About twenty minutes later Lieutenant Salvas looked into the scope and saw that they were bringing two more machine guns into the same locations. He got on the phone and said, "Have you changed the range of those guns?" The reply was no, and he added, "Do you want to send some more rounds? They are setting up more machine guns." They said they would, after the Germans had a little time to get settled. They sent in six, lowered the guns slightly, and sent in six more. We saw no more activity.

We liked our position. The sun was at our backs, so I would not be filming into it. They would be looking into the sun and would not be able to see us too well. The barrage started and it made for ideal photography. I could hear the shells coming over and started the camera before they hit. I was getting close-up scenes of the bursts with the long lens.

At abour four o'clock the infantry started across. We did not get all of the machine guns. I could see the bullets hitting the water. The men were in about three feet of water. The bullets were hitting the poor guys. It was pretty bad. They crossed and lost a lot of good men.

It was getting dark. Lieutenant Salvas and I followed the wire out and returned to the road and our jeep. At the command post the colonel was still there. He said, "Would you guys like to come and eat with us?" We replied that we had no mess kits, to which he answered, "That's all right, I'll furnish you with mess kits." We followed him back and were eating dinner. He approached us and asked for our names, rank, and serial numbers. I said to him, "Why do you want that? What have we done wrong?" "Nothing," he replied. "You boys have done such a splendid job today that I am going to put you in for the Bronze Star."

We often talked about those two spotters who were killed.

—Sergeant Barney Caliendo

Liberté, Egalité, Fraternité

IN THE SPRING of 1944 thousands of American troops were temporarily stationed in Northern Ireland before transport to England and the activation of the Third Army. The 166th Photo Company was billeted in Maxwell Manor, a large estate near Bangor. The personnel of the photo units was finalized there, and consequently many men were companions in the same unit in the ensuing campaign in France and Germany. The units usually consisted of a lieutenant in charge, two motion picture cameramen, two still photographers, and two drivers.

In one such unit the motion picture cameramen, Sgt. Theodore W. Sizer and Sgt. William E. Teas, were also excellent still photographers. They brought extensive civilian photographic experience to the army, which they used effectively to determine the assignment of their unit to the Second French Armored Division. Their officer recognized their capabilities and supported their collaboration.

While we were stationed in the little fishing village of Groomsport, Northern Ireland, our weekends were primarily our own, which we could squander roving the lush, green countryside—unless we were stuck with guard or KP duty. On one such weekend Sergeant Sizer discovered Waringstown, and therein Mr. Hunter, the headmaster of the school. Mr. Hunter was an accomplished raconteur, and authority on the history of Ireland, and specifically on the history of Waringstown. The original settlement had consisted of a colony of Flemish weavers who had been imported to Ireland by Lord Waring. For many years all the royal linens in Buckingham Palace had been woven in Waringstown. The town had many shuttle looms, and as a child walking to school Mr. Hunter could tell by the shuttle pattern what was being woven: napkins, sheets, pillows, and so forth.

One Sunday, when Mr. Hunter was taking us on a personal tour of the town, I was impressed by Lady Waring's beautiful estate, a stately old structure in the Flemish style, with clusters of fluted chimneys and carefully tended grounds surrounded by yew hedges. I was fascinated with the old-world atmosphere of the place, and I asked Mr. Hunter if he would try to get me permission to photograph the property. Mr. Hunter answered that it might be difficult to arrange, but that he would try.

The following weekend he said that he had been successful with his inquiry, and that I might proceed with my project whenever I wished. The day we chose was perfect, with brilliant blue sky cluttered with marshmallow cumulus clouds. The only handicap we were under was an occasional spatter of raindrops which never lasted long, but threatened to damage our camera and therefore sent us scampering for temporary shelter. One of these minor cloudbursts caught us in front of a low portico that protected the front door. Sergeant Sizer, who had taught the subject of English history in civilian life and was an expert on antiques, remarked that he would just about give anything to see the interior. As though on cue, the door opened and a lady in maid's uniform said that Lady Waring would like us to have tea and crumpets with her.

Lady Waring was a frail woman, clad entirely in black. She was a perfect hostess, and after tea, took us on a thorough personal tour of the house. Sergeant Sizer was delighted with the experience and Lady Waring was obviously appreciative of his understanding and knowledge. Then it was back to wielding the old Speed Graphic and touring the rest of the estate, including the private chapel.

In civilian life I had been a commercial and portrait photographer in Pasadena, California. As a hobby pursuit, I had done considerable photographic salon exhibiting. When I enlisted in the army I was reluctant to abandon this endeavor for the duration of the war, so I had packed the major component materials and transported them, first to Camp Crowder, and then overseas with our regular issue of supplies. The photographs of the Waring Estate provided the perfect opportunity to take advantage of my foresight.

By rigging a light bulb in a five-pound rations can and adapting the versatile Speed Graphic with a glass sandwich negative carrier, I was able to make a Mickey Mouse, expedient horizontal enlarger. Being without a darkroom, the device could only operate at night when all the lights were out in our Quonset hut. The resulting prints were washed in the mess hall, dried, split-toned, redried, and mounted with dry mounting tissue on 16 × 20 mat board.

I selected six of the best photographs of the Waring Estate and presented them to Mr. Hunter to give to Lady Waring. The following week Mr. Hunter informed us that Lady Waring would like us to be her guests at a cricket match the following Sunday. It was not until we arrived there that we discovered the whole story.

The townspeople were agog at the appearance of Lady Waring and the American soldiers. It seems that Mr. Hunter's disclaimer when he said that the photographs might be difficult to arrange had a solid basis in fact. Lord Waring had died several months earlier and Lady Waring had since his death become a recluse, never leaving her estate and having no more visitors than business dictated. Although I had no substantiation of this, I like to believe that Ted Sizer's appreciation of her worldly treasures and the documentation of the beauties of her

estate in my photographs led her to reenter the world, albeit the frac-
tured world of war.

We remained in Ireland several months, but with the impending
activation of the Third Army we were shipped to England and were
attached to the Twentieth Corps near Manchester.

—Sergeant William E. Teas

WHEN WE WERE IN MANCHESTER in the Twentieth Corps with not
much to do, in April of 1944 before the invasion, Teas got the idea of
photographing some of the generals. We went to the signal corps staff
officer and asked him, and he responded to go ahead. Arrangements
were made, and we went to a general's house and found him with his
bullterrier, which he wanted in the picture. Both he and the terrier had
very strong, rather protruding eyes. When we left I said to Sergeant
Teas that we were never going to get anything out of those shots because both the bullterrier and the general were going to look like they
were pop-eyed. Sergeant Teas said that he would sepia-tint them. This
softened the eyes down, and the pictures were very nice. We showed
them to the general and he liked them.

During that time I had been talking to General LeClerc about being
in the French army. I had heard about the French army being trained
in England, and I was curious. Under the general's verbal orders we
were directed to go to Yorkshire. There we met the French division.

The organization was entirely different from what we were accustomed to in the American army. It was very unstructured—a mecca for
Frenchmen with travel all over England. They had hundreds and hundreds of people who were not even on the payroll. They were milling
about and driving the trucks and acting very busy. A disparate bunch:
some were North Africans; some were people who had left Paris and
gone into Vichy France; others had made their way to Portugal. All
had eventually escaped to England and had gotten into this Charles de
Gaulle military organization. A great many were in constant trouble.
The stockade was very busy.

We were one of only a few American units in the encampment. The
other units were there to assist in future tactical liaisons with Allied
forces. The division had no cameramen, and I felt that being with
Frenchmen in the liberation of their homeland would make for some
significant photography. I suggested this to our photo officer, who
made the request, and we were transferred and assigned to the Second
French Armored Division.

—Sergeant Theodore W. Sizer

WHEN WE GOT INTO THE FRENCH ARMY in England in 1944 we had no idea of the adventures ahead of us. The immediate contrasts to the American army were apparent. The first distinction occurred when Cpl. Francis Wagner and the rest of our PFCs and corporals had to get used to returning salutes, since all NCOs in the French army are considered officers. After the novelty of returning salutes palled, the gesture became passé, because in the French army the return of a salute by an officer is not mandatory. In the French army the noncoms, called *sous-officiers,* were served meals in the officers' mess, ate upon ceramic plates, and used silverware—a real contrast to the metal mess kits we were accustomed to. Also, the French had brought with them from Morocco thousands of gallons of red wine, served as generously as water at lunch and dinner. Hundreds of red-fezzed spahi troops were on permanent guard and KP duty.

The *comme ci, comme ça* attitude of the French served our unit well when we embarked for the Channel crossing from Bournemouth on August 1. We were assigned to an LST (landing ship tank), with all our equipment already aboard, when we noticed three Red Cross Clubmobiles being loaded on an LST beside ours. There were real, live Red Cross women with doughnuts and coffee. This was the first consignment of Red Cross women to cross the Channel in the Normandy sector. We requested of our French officer that, although we were assigned to cross in one ship, we would rather embark on a neighboring craft. No problem, was his response, just change ships. This unregimented flexibility afforded us a leisurely, picnicking atmosphere in crossing the Channel. The ladies loaned us bathing trunks and we had a pleasant, Malibu-type beach party just offshore France, with southern California weather to accompany it.

Our first night in Normandy was spent in a bombed-out school building beside a road upon which tanks traveled inland, and we tried to sleep in spite of the metal clanking and squealing. It was there in the late afternoon that Sergeant Sizer inaugurated his clean-table policy. Somewhere in the rubble he had found an unshattered desk. He cleaned it off and arranged all of his toilet articles and personal possessions on it. He announced to all present that this was his personal table, and woe be to anyone who placed anything on his table or disarranged the contents. This policy was maintained throughout the war— his way of clinging to a little order in the midst of chaos. As the dark descended, our little eighteen-year-old paisano (civilian interpreter) Angeline rushed up to Sizer and said, "Sergeant Sizer, where's the toilet?" Sizer made a sweeping, grandiloquent gesture and answered with dramatic flourish, "Angeline, from here on in it is all toilet."

When we were near Saint-Lô, Sergeant Sizer decided to photograph the return of soldiers to their homes. Many Frenchmen had been in exile for years, with no contact with homes or families. He insisted that the photography be real, with no staging of or influencing the participants.

Two officers were found who lived nearby, and in two jeeps we started out. One officer lived in a small village outside of Saint-Lô. His house was intact. We drove up, parked, and found his wife and children there. We filmed a joyous, emotional reunion. Still pictures by Corporal James of the meeting and accompanying caption information appeared in an article in *Time* magazine.

The second officer lived in Saint-Lô. We encountered many prominent signs as we entered the city, which emphatically stated that the city was "Off Limits" to all troops. We barreled blithely along through the devastation. Shells of buildings were surrounded by piles of rubble, remnants of the artillery and air bombardments poured into the battle for Saint-Lô.

He first directed us to a cemetery. He had been brought up by grandparents and would see if they had survived. The cemetery was extensively cratered by shell fire, and the tombstones on his family plot had been obliterated leaving only depressions. His house was in a less damaged part of the city. The front door was unlocked. Our translator could hear the conversation of the officers, and kept us informed.

"Germans have been occupying the house. There is a picture of Hitler on the wall of a room upstairs." A window flew open and a framed picture of the *der Führer* flew out and landed near the house. We waited alertly for the next move, cameras focused and ready. At that moment a jeep came charging up the hill on the road toward us, with a large MP master sergeant in the front seat. He started to yell before the vehicle stopped.

"What the hell are you guys doing here? Don't you know this is Off Limits? Get the hell out of here." "Calm down. Be quiet," I called out. "We are doing a photo assignment. I will explain in a minute." "You will explain right now," he yelled as he jumped out of his jeep and confronted me. "Here is my SHAEF pass," I countered, slamming it down on the hood of our jeep. "It gives us permission to take photos anywhere." He looked at it and responded furiously. "Do you think this thing is from God himself?" he demanded. "If it was, would you recognize your Father's signature?" I replied, making mental note that it was the best comeback of my lifetime.

At that moment the French officers came out of the house. "In your jeeps, and follow me, I'm taking you out of Saint-Lô, and stay out," was the MP's parting shout. As we followed, the officer explained that the house had not been used by his grandparents for a long time. None of their possessions were there, nor was there any clue about their fate, or location.

By reason of General Patton's audacious armored thrusts west and north to Chambois during the third week in August, thousands of Germans were trapped in the Falaise Gap sector. It was the first time Allied command had complete control. Near us, Poles, Canadians, and the French commanded the heights above the valley. There were two panzer divisions holed up in the valley. We could walk right out on the hills and watch the action. The Germans did not fire back. They got blasted. Every once in a while a tank would try to make a run for it. It was like a shooting gallery. We were near observation scopes, ones with high magnification, and Sizer asked me, "If I put my camera lens up against the scope lens, would I get anything?" I replied that the optics would be different, it would not work, it was not practical. He tried it, and the later critique described the results as excellent.

An armistice was arranged to enable Germans to surrender. Corporal James and I went down in the valley to a little town and found a dozen Americans from the 8th Infantry. They had been pinned down there all night and were waiting for the armistice in order to get out. They had captured a German payroll truck and had stacks of francs in bound packets. At that time the American army prohibited French francs as legal tender for GIs. We had those small invasion francs that were issued to us. So the men were saying, "Take a pack of this, and a pack of that, load up with one thousand franc notes." I said no, I would just take one of each as souvenirs. I shot scenes of them lighting cigars with franc notes.

Three days later the American command announced that thereafter French francs were legal tender for GIs. I could have gone into Paris a wealthy man.

—Sergeant Aaron Lubitsch

WHEN WE GOT TO FRANCE the French division had American divisions on either flank. Communication and tactical cooperation between the French and the Americans was very desirable as they moved down roads and encountered enemy resistance, but the French were inclined to ignore this. They fought along at their own pace, as though the flanking Allies did not exist. This was infuriating to the American liaison teams. It was dangerous for us and maddening when we went out to film action, because there was no information for us as to where the action was to take place, what the objectives were, and when it would begin. With the French, even when you had a war on you took a couple of hours out in the middle of the day to have lunch. The war would stop until they wanted to have something going on.

There were compensations. We never had to worry about housing when we were with the French. They always arranged for us to stay in somebody's house. We were never out in the field, sleeping on the ground in a slit trench. We always had good meals. When we were not in combat it was a rollicking good time.

In one village we were quartered in a house with a lovely old lady, who had been a child in the first world war and remembered the fighting. So deaf she could hardly communicate, she nonetheless was aware of current events. She had her private way of protesting the presence of the German garrison when they were in the town. In her small embroidery, which she worked on every day, she had woven a small American flag and a French tricolor—a secret flaunting of her indomitable spirit. The young lady of the house was terribly sad. Her husband had recently died. A member of the FFI (the French Forces of the Interior), he had participated in sabotage to assist the arrival of the French division. The Germans had caught him and killed him along with his compatriots.

I was very upset at the French treatment of the German SS prisoners. They would surrender and then would be beaten up and frequently killed. The young Jewish man who was our interpreter explained the reason for this. The SS were especially cruel and vicious in their treatment of the civilian population during the years of occupation. He had recently learned that his two sisters, along with many children in a village school, had been executed by the SS because they were Jewish. When the French captured the SS, they acted upon long memories of persecution and cruel treatment.

—Sergeant Theodore W. Sizer

WE WERE TO DISCOVER that the French were daring fighters, filled with élan and esprit de corps, along with other laudable qualities. What they lacked most was organization and discipline. After landing in France, we ran into an American liaison group who had been assigned to the division. They were wailing about their fate and complained there was no rapport between their endeavors and their counterparts on the French staff.

A few months later this same group was responsible for the destruction of two brand-new Tiger tanks, which were descending from railroad flatcars that had brought them from Germany to France. For their accomplishment the men were awarded the Croix de Guerre. We were assigned to photograph the award ceremony and were surprised to find the same crew, which previously had been so unhappy with their assignment, celebrating around their vehicle, drinking champagne, and carrying on in the height of elation.

"Does that award mean so much to you?" I inquired of the CO. He stopped celebrating long enough to reply, "We don't give a damn about the award. We are celebrating because we got our orders transferring us to an American division."

The American PI (photo interpretation group), whose job it was to interpret aerial photos for enemy vehicles, had similar complaints. Their briefings with the French were either disbelieved or ignored. Our unit made the habit of checking with the Americans for impending combat locations.

Frequently the French would misinterpret commands from officers. When ordered to camouflage their vehicles, instead of the muddy brown and green colored burlap netting, they used the brightly colored fluorescent banners used to mark fields with drop zones for aircraft.

Our advance from Normandy eastward was steady, with our division benefiting from Patton's rampaging armored divisions adjacent to us. As we neared Paris the decision was made to allow (for political reasons) the Second French Armored Division to precede the Americans into the city. After three days of sloughing through constant rain that made roads and fields a soggy mire, our division awoke to clear, crisp blue skies and brilliant sunlight.

We moved fairly rapidly through the suburbs near Porte de Saint-Cloud until the streets became a hazard of curb-to-curb celebrants. Our first event happened as we were halted in our creeping advance. An elderly French women shouted an unintelligible phrase at us from the second-story balcony of her apartment. She was holding aloft a brown paper bag. Obviously she intended to throw it to us. We nodded assent to her, with "Ouis" of agreement. She tossed her package and it landed on target between us. A war correspondent in a jeep behind us rushed up and inquired, "What is it?" A quick investigation revealed it was about a pound of white granular sugar, a product that the army was in no need of but which the owner must have scrimped and hoarded for many months to obtain in German-occupied France. The correspondent jogged along beside us long enough to jot down our names and addresses. A couple of weeks later James received a clipping from a Niagara Falls newspaper. His hometown had published the story.

Suddenly our roster increased. A young French student introduced himself as Jacques Menier and offered his services as interpreter. As he spoke excellent English we accepted and piled him aboard our burdened vehicle. His assistance was invaluable in the forthcoming weeks.

The closer we got to the major intersection of Porte de Saint-Cloud the heavier the traffic of shouting, cheering pedestrians. However, the traffic ahead seemed to be thinning, and the shouting suddenly became screams as people scrambled to the doorways for protection. A small German contingent had arrived and was setting up a roadblock. The advance jeeps of our column, ours included, were moved into a courtyard of a *mairie* precinct. We spent about fifteen minutes there until the miniature uprising was summarily overcome. There was a BBC correspondent there, and because we were the first Americans he had seen, he wound up his tape with an interview of me and signed off. The time was 8:25 A.M., August 25, the morning of the liberation of Paris.

We had barely gotten back on the street when an overexuberant celebrant lofted a magnum of champagne from the curb. It could have bashed a face had not James deflected it. It landed near the gear shift, and fortunately did not break. Since there was no casualty the throng was delighted and the participant took bows when I hoisted the bottle in his direction as a gesture of thanks. A couple of blocks farther his largess was topped as two brawny Frenchmen came running out of a corner bistro, barging their way across the street, and deposited a full case of champagne in our jeep.

I had been constantly checking the scene behind us and decided that this was the time to make my move to record the celebration. As James pulled out of the traffic route and parked beside the curb, I stood up in the jeep and panned my Eymo movie camera across the mass of cheering people, with the French tanks and half-tracks looming in the background. Then I abandoned our vehicle and dashed into a doorway and up a flight of stairs to an apartment with a balcony overlooking the scene. It turned out to be the headquarters for the FFI. After a quick toast of champagne I was beginning to feel that his gesture was the equivalent of an American handshake. I adjourned to the balcony and shot ample footage of the military convoy creeping its way through the cheering mob. I thanked my hosts and started back to my jeep, but the Frenchmen anticipated my departure and hoisting me up on their shoulders proceeded to carry me to my jeep. I felt like a football coach whose team had just won the Superbowl. However, they were carrying me away from my transportation, not toward it. This minor difficulty overcome, they deposited me beside a lovely French mademoiselle, who was talking with James in perfect English, with "zee" charming accent.

She was about five foot nine and blond with blue eyes and a Holland-type blouse, and what in the States would be called a Veronica Lake hairdo. As a matter of fact her facial features were quite similar to Hollywood's Miss Lake. She handed me a card. On it was printed Margot de la Croix, with the simple word *Actrice,* and a Porte de Saint-Cloud address and phone number.

"We would like you," she said, tapping the card, "to have dinner weez us tonight." I smiled at her, and replied, "I'm afraid I will be too busy the next few days for any social life. I will certainly take you up on the invitation as soon as possible, if it still applies." "But, of course." I glanced at the rather frail, blond man beside her, who had been smiling and nodding as we conversed. He obviously did not understand English and agreed with everything he heard.

"Your brother?" I asked. She shook her head negatively. "Your husband?" "Oui." But her eyes implied, "Don't let it bother you." He offered me a limp hand and muttered, "Bernard." Her eyes implied correctly. In a few days she became my close companion for two romantic weeks.

We were off to the Arc de Triomphe looming ahead. When we reached the arch a small garrison of German soldiers had just surrendered and was being marched under it, hands clasped on heads, as a few gendarmes made feeble efforts to restrain civilians from hitting them with umbrellas, fists, and any weapon at hand. After filming this, I started down the Champs-Élyseés toward the Place de la Concorde. Street fighting could be seen and sporadic gunfire heard several blocks away.

I had proceeded perhaps a hundred yards when an arm reached out of a gateway and unceremoniously hauled me into a courtyard. Here a French newsreel unit was set up for film and sound recording. It was an elaborate piece of gear, all chrome and shiny, with a few attachments unfamiliar to me. Recently there have been revelations of early television experiments during the liberation of Paris, and I often wondered if I could have been televised as early as 1944.

The purpose was an interview, but there was one small problem. I did not speak French, and none of the crew spoke any English. A dapper little Frenchman in a business suit volunteered his services as an interpreter, and the session began. The crew would ask a question, the interpreter would translate it to me, I would answer in English, the translator would interpret in French, and so forth. It was a prolonged process, and when it was finished the translator grasped my hand effusively and asked if I would accompany him home to meet his wife and daughter. He was a Parisian banker and lived across the Champs-Élyseés. I felt indebted for his help in recording and agreed to a short visit with his family.

Fortunately the elevator was working, for most of Paris was off power that day and my new ''ami'' lived in a penthouse apartment. Introductions were in order and then the inevitable champagne toast. After the toast to the United States and France, my host surprised me by his next statement.

''And now, monsieur, I would like to offer you, in all sincerity, anything you desire. If there is anything I can do for you, or give you, just say the word. Money, anything.'' I didn't need money. I was a nonsmoker. Cigarettes were selling for twenty dollars a carton. I had been saving my rations of one carton a week from the French army and one from the American army, and of course I had my full sergeant's pay. During the past few weeks in the rush for Paris we had bypassed several shower points.

I replied, ''I would like a bath.'' My benefactor shook his head negatively and said, ''Very sorry, monsieur, but in Paris today there is no hot water.'' ''Well,'' I replied, ''I will take a cold bath.'' The lavish but chilled bath was prepared and just as I stepped into the tub I glanced at my image in the mirror, and was surprised to see a red beard. Scraping with my fingernails, I found it caked with lipstick. I left the bath ten pounds lighter than when I had entered, profusely thanked my host, and departed.

Rendezvousing with James and Jacques and the jeep, we decided to head for the Hôtel Scribe in order to catch the early courier service, which would take our footage to London for processing. Several streets around the hotel were still roadblocked, but Jacques knew the territory well, and we arrived by a circuitous route, employing several narrow alleys.

A U.S. first lieutenant had more or less taken over the hotel in the name of the United States Army. We were the second group of Americans to arrive. I requested a room, and the lieutenant inquired as to my outfit. I replied the Second French Armored Division. We were given a key, and we repaired to our rooms to organize our film, fill out captions, and so forth. Then we rested to get ready for the ordeal of the liberation parade the following day.

—Sergeant William E. Teas

AT THE END OF THE FIRST DAY of the liberation in Paris we found ourselves at Place des Invalides looking for a place to spend the night. Most importantly, we needed a place to conceal our jeep. Stealing of and from American vehicles had been a continual problem as we traveled across France. We met a young man who spoke English very well, who invited us to stay at his house, which had a building where our vehicle would be safe. It was a beautiful home, not far from des Invalides. We met his mother who also spoke English very well, as her grandmother was English. We discovered they had very little food, so we shared chopped ham and egg yolk cans from our C rations, and cigarettes, which were very valuable to them to barter for necessities.

I wondered what had happened to Paris fashions. Before the German occupation, Parisian fashions had always been in the news. I asked her what I might learn about this. I felt the people at home would be interested in that sort of thing, and it was a change from the grimness of what we had been photographing.

She called up her couturier. He said, yes, we could come down and meet with him. The next morning we did so. He had his models all dressed in the latest styles. We were the only people in the Grand Salon. Because of our equipment we had to do the photography outside. We took about ten of the models and posed them around the jeep. Then we took some of them to other locations for scenic backgrounds. It was very interesting, and we shot a lot of pictures. When I took them to the photo officer he sputtered, "There is a war going on, and *you* are shooting French fashions?"

In Paris during the first days of liberation there was continual harassment by the collaborators. Armed with a ragtag assortment of weapons, there were pockets of them firing away all over the city. These were Frenchmen, who over the years of occupation, either by conviction or expediency, became active assistants to the Germans. They cooperated in many ways, including revealing the identity of their countrymen who were members of the FFI to the SS. Those betrayed were tortured and shot. The German soldiers in Paris wanted to surrender, but the collaborators were afraid. We saw truckloads of them being hauled away. We photographed many of them. Civilians by the roadside yelled and jeered at the Frenchmen in the trucks. A woman beside me was especially vociferous, shouting and shaking her fist.

The collaborators were very active the day of liberation when General de Gaulle arrived in the city. They were at home with the gargoyles in Notre Dame Cathedral when he made his dramatic visit to the historic structure. His presence with the current joyous release from bondage invoked epochs of glorious French history.

The area in front of the cathedral was jammed with civilians, soldiers, and military tanks and half-tracks. When General de Gaulle appeared, the collaborators began to shoot from their lofty perch. Immediately the troops began to shoot upward. Machine gun and rifle fire created a veritable rain of marble chips and dust from the intricate decorations on the venerable Gothic facade of the structure.

De Gaulle did not hesitate. Ignoring the firing he turned and strode through the grand central portal and down the central aisle, followed by his retinue. There was shooting from the lofts within the church. The audience jumped up in panic from their seats and rushed to the protection of the side aisles. Without looking left or right, with bullets hitting beside him, de Gaulle walked straight down the center aisle. When he got to the front he sat down in front of the altar. Through it all the "Te Deum" was sung in the background.

After several weeks in Paris the division continued the war. In Paris a great number of men in the division decided to leave—they would just resign. For them, Paris was liberated; the war was over. New people wanted to join, so they were enlisted. They had no training, so when the division left it was a very different one than had entered the city. When we got into combat they knew nothing about fighting.

The French division went as far as the German border. There it stopped, while the Allies proceeded to fight in Germany. We transferred to the U.S. 80th Division. After that it was tough. Patton moved systematically and thoroughly. It got tough. It was very tough.

—Sergeant Theodore W. Sizer

WHEN WE LEFT THE FRENCH DIVISION our departure was not celebrated by dancing in the streets. Although we made many friends in our associations, the differences of the spiritual attitudes between the French and American troops were obvious. The French possessed indomitable spirit in fighting for the liberation of their homeland. Americans were involved in a less personally inspired war. Every objective obtained, at uncomfortable cost, brought them farther from home in time and miles. This was a grimmer, more desperate confrontation, and the war became more personal and unpleasant.

—Sergeant William E. Teas

Sgt. William E. Teas

"I WAS IMPRESSED by Lady Waring's beautiful estate, a stately old structure in the Flemish style, with clusters of fluted chimneys, and carefully tended grounds surrounded by yew hedges."

Sgt. William E. Te

"THE DAY WE CHOSE was perfect with brilliant blue sky cluttered with marshmallow cumulus clouds. The only handicap we were under was an occasional spatter of raindrops, which never lasted long."

"THEN IT WAS BACK to wielding the old Speed Graphic and touring the rest of the estate, including the private chapel."

Sgt. William E. Teas

Lt. Adrien Sa[...]

A PATROL ENTERING SAINT-LÔ. The two-week battle for Saint-Lô was vicious and deadly. It was captured July 18 by a battalion of the 29th Division, led by Maj. Tom Howie. When he was killed, his troops carried his body into the city, where his coffin was respectfully placed upon a pile of building rubble, and he became immortalized as the "Major of Saint-Lô." Two weeks later Third Army tanks punched out of the hedgerows and routed the Germans at Avranches.

Sgt. William E. Teas

ON THE STEPS of the Sacré Cour in Paris, men and women of the French Freedom Fighters, the clandestine FFI, enjoy public recognition during the liberation, August 25, 1944.

IN THE BOIS DE BOULOGNE actress Margot de la Croix, translator and companion to the author, William E. Teas, posed in the momentous days following the liberation of Paris.

Sgt. William E. Teas

166th Signal Photo

THE LIBERATION OF PARIS was substantially complete when on liberation day the army vehicles slowly moved through the jubilant crowds and arrived at the monument to Napoleonic military triumphs—the Arc de Triomphe.

Sgt. Ralph Butterfield

RUSSIAN SOLDIERS RELAX with proprietary complacency in Prague during May of 1945. American tanks were first into the city and, to the extreme disappointment of the majority of the Czechs, were required by Allied command, for political reasons, to retreat and open the city to Russian occupation.

Maizieres-les-Metz

WITH INCREASED DEMAND for photographic coverage and an insufficient number of officers to supervise, experienced noncommissioned officers were placed in charge of photo teams. Sgt. Russell A. Meyer was given command of a photo unit consisting of two photographers, a driver, and a jeep. Having access to division war tents, which contained large situation maps covered with a plastic sheet that marked the position of fighting units, Sergeant Meyer decided that a sector eight miles north of Metz was appropriate for film coverage.

There, at Maizieres-les-Metz, two battalions of the 90th Division had been fighting for twenty-seven days to capture the small mill town. The slag piles at the north and south end of the main street, which was lined with stone houses, provided unusual terrain for the German defense and American attacks.

Sergeants Meyer and Butterfield filmed mop-up actions during the last days of the battle.

In the early afternoon at the Herman Goering Steel Mill at Maizieres-les-Metz, the somber gray clouds were so low and dark it seemed like twilight. The sprawling mill was eerily inactive, with neither moving cables overhead parading the ore buckets nor customary heat shimmering atop the towering brick chimneys.

A slag pile stretched toward the town, its contours of sterile, brown heaps a progression of dumpings. Sergeant Meyer and I rode along the road paralleling the pile, cramped in the backseat of a jeep. A captain in the front turned to our driver, and with a wry grin said, "When you pass the rubble from that bridge at this end of the pile let your clutch out, we're under observation. See the corner down there just this side of the knocked-out tank? Make for that and turn sharp left."

We were jostled as the jeep heaved and rolled passing over rubble and were forced back against our seats by the acceleration. The captain turned his head away from the wind pressure and shouted at us in the back, "I had an OP [observation post] on the edge of the pile, but we had to move it—too exposed, the shell fragments ricocheted all over the slag. Nothing to stop them."

As we neared the corner the jeep slowed momentarily, the outside tires squealing faintly as they rounded the corner and passed the tank. The gutted turret had scorched the white star beneath it, and a track was stretched out upon the darkened road. We accelerated again past a picket fence in front of a row of houses. On a porch a nondescript GI squatted against a wall, the litter from a K ration balanced on his lap. His head suddenly jerked up from his canteen cup, and his gaze intently followed the jeep. There was a red spurt on the roadside a dozen yards from the jeep, and an explosion and a burst of pure white phosphorus smoke puffed and balled upward in a soaring cloud.

As the soldier on the porch grabbed his rations and quickly stepped through the doorway, we bent over and the captain shouted, "Go! Turn in at the second tree on your right. Not here! Farther! In here! In here!" The jeep swerved away from the road between two houses, stopped by a wall, and we scrambled out. On the road behind them, following the smoke shell, one then a second mortar exploded. The captain eyed us knowingly as he led us across a porch and into a house.

"Wait here, I'll be back in a few minutes," he said as he went down a stairway in the next room. The driver, Cpl. Charles Sumners, went outside, and Sgt. Russell Meyer and I squatted on our heels next to the wall. Four men across the room looked at us with brief curiosity. Red crosses were painted on white patches on the front of their helmets, and soiled, creased Red Cross arm bands were wrapped around their sleeves above their elbows. They spoke quietly with one another in short, abrupt sentences, and in moments of silence, waited and listened.

There was an increasing hiss in the air outside, climaxed by the explosion of a mortar shell nearby. The door flew open and was momentarily blocked as Corporal Sumners and a second GI tried to squeeze through the doorway together. They heaved and burst into the room simultaneously, glancing sheepishly at the others.

Voices below grew louder, and the captain came up the stairs with other officers. He remarked to the waiting men, "Okay, now I'll show you the OP." We went into the yard where Meyer and I lifted our camera cases from the jeep as the captain continued, "Your driver stays here with the vehicle. Better stay inside the house, it's ventilated but better than out here." Corporal Sumners laughed, looking at the broken windows and the smashed wall, then shoved his hands into his jacket pockets as he went up the steps and inside.

The officer led us around the side of the building into a garden. We walked rapidly, in single file, keeping close together. The even rows of vegetables were broken by spattered depressions of explosions. The path led under trees, through a fence, and along a brick wall. Loose mortar, jarred from the top, was strewn along the pathway. It was quiet again, except for the snap of rifle shots in the distance. We came out into an open space beside a railroad embankment. Four men were lying along its crest, a dozen yards apart, manning machine guns poked beneath the rails. One was looking at a *Stars and Stripes* and finishing balled it up and with his head low tossed it to the next man, the paper bouncing on the rock ballast.

We walked parallel with the railroad embankment. On the right the bulk of the ore smelter dominated the area, blackened and sooty with the veneer of years of smoke. The railroad tracks ran between the smelter and a long, two-storied building, whose plastered walls were chipped and scarred with shrapnel grooves. The roof was marred by broken tiles and smashed holes. All the windows were broken, the sashes of some knocked out entirely.

"That's the OP, " said the captain, with continuing joviality, "you understand I take no responsibility if the roof falls in." He led us into the mill, jumping down a four-foot wall to the level under the smelter. We copied his movements, setting down our cases for support as we jumped, pulling them off after we walked under a concrete passageway.

A hallway ran the length of the building, with doors opening into the rooms on both sides. As we walked toward a stairway at the far end, our feet crunched upon broken glass and several inches of litter. Each room had been ransacked, the contents of the drawers and cabinets strewn upon the floors and into the hall. The papers, a foot deep in some of the rooms, were packed down and dirty. The stairs ascended to a hallway, similar to the one below, and the captain led us to one of the middle rooms, where we set down our cases.

Five men were standing in varying degrees of proximity and attention to an open window. With neither glass nor sash, it faced a row of stone houses. One of the men held a telephone to his ear, his hand resting on his shoulder, head leaning on the earpiece, his body drooping wearily. He glanced at us momentarily as we entered, then looked out the window as he continued into the receiver, ". . . elevation three zero, deflection four zero. Yeah. They were a little high," he paused and continued, "the church and the building this way. Wait, let's see, south of the church. Anytime." His tone was casual, the sentences without beginning and ending inflection.

The other men gazed intently out the window, moving warily around the open space in front of it, keeping well back in the darkness of the room. The captain stepped over to the wall beside the opening, knelt, and glanced at us as he nodded his head outside.

"You see those humps on the ground fifty yards out there? A few Germans are in a dugout there. See the wood barracks just to the right? There are some in the basement of that. See that first stone building this side of the church? They have an OP on the top floor we are going to try and get."

We looked out. The barracks across four sets of railroad tracks was a two-storied frame building. Beyond it was a street and next to it a row of stone houses with tile roofs. At the left a church steeple had large chunks knocked out of the spire where a shell explosion had battered it. Smoke and heat waves rose from a fire in a building next to the church—the sharp, confident crackling indicating a new flame.

Sergeant Meyer, the captain, and I withdrew into the hallway, and he looked at us quizzically. "Thanks, captain," said Sergeant Meyer. "We will get shots of explosions on the barracks." "Don't take too long," the captain replied. "This is an uncomfortable place at night." We took our cameras from the cases and wound them tightly. "We should get good footage of the explosions, we are so close," said Sergeant Meyer, as he fitted a long tubular lens into his camera. He continued, "I'll use this ten-inch lens which should edit well with your two inch."

We returned to the room, and I spoke to the officer with the telephone. "Will you let us know when you are going to fire the barrage, Sir?" The observer looked at me curiously, and countered with, "What have you got there?" "Cameras, movie cameras. We would like to film some of the shelling from the window." The officer looked wryly at his men, who smiled at his nonplussed expression.

He spoke into the mouthpiece, "Joe, Joe? Say, uh," he paused, looking at the men again, smiling at their interest, "start with six rounds. Some photographers are here. Photographers. Gosh. I don't know, *Stars and Stripes* I guess." He listened, chuckled, and turned to us. "He wants to know if they will be in the *Denver Post*." "They are movies, for newsreels. Maybe they will go to Denver and be at the Bijou." The officer spoke again into the phone, "Joe, Joe. They are motion pictures. Yeah. He is not taking us. He wants mortar burst on the target. The *Denver Post* will look a lot better without your puss on it anyway." He listened for a moment, and turned to us. "He's going to get C and D companies, too, and a cannon company. You should have plenty to see. I'll let you know when they are on the way."

While Sergeant Meyer went into the next room, I went over to the wall and slowly moved my camera into the corner of the window, resting it upon a ledge. In my viewfinder I framed the barracks building. There was the faint sound of evenly spaced, dull explosions, the "spud" of mortars leaving the tubes. A faint whisper in the air spoke of their flight, and I pressed the shutter release, the camera whining and clicking. Explosions whammed in rapid succession. Dust and smoke spurted from the building framed within the viewfinder. When the spring wound down I rewound quickly, reframed, and continued the filming. Sharper, more jarring explosions from the cannon company mixed with the mortar barrage. The spurting dust became a dense cloud that drifted to the OP, rose into the air, and obscured all the buildings, concealing them from additional filming.

Backing away from the window and into the hallway, I squatted against the wall, opened the camera, and took out the film reel. As I reloaded the camera and ran it to check the film loops before seating and locking the cover into position, one of the GIs, restlessly prowling, stopped, watched intently, and squatted next to me. He spoke with a companionable, comfortable drawl.

"You know, I had a little camera when I was home. Jest a box camera, and I took a lot of pictures and printed them myself. Took up the whole kitchen when I was printing. Jest pictures of my nieces, and aunts and uncles. They turned out pretty good, too. Are you from *Stars and Stripes?*" "Army Pictorial Service," I replied. "What's that?'' ''Same thing, practically,'' I said. The GI continued, ''I found a camera a while ago, and took out the lens. I thought maybe I could use it some day, put it in a camera, or something. I have it here, kinda wrapped in a sock. Is it any . . .,'' he stopped talking and listened. We both ducked and covered our heads as a faint whistle increased in volume, ending with a swish and explosion on the coal pile behind the building. Fragments and loose coal rattled on the roof.

''Mortar?'' ''Too big for a mortar. They have been trying to find us all day.'' He hitched his rifle to a shoulder and went into a room. I slipped the camera into the case, snapped the lids, and joined Sergeant Meyer in the room with the officer and the telephone.

The upper floor of the building was almost crowded now, as other men arrived. Men walked from room to room, peering out windows then returning to the hallway in a continuous, restless movement. From the end of the hallway, where a machine gun pointed down the tracks, a young soldier, a dirty shawl sticking up almost nattily from his begrimed collar, hurried into the room and tapped the observer on the shoulder. He spoke urgently, ''Sir, about three Jerries are crossing the tracks down by the Y. I can see them with the naked eye.''

The officer at the phone was talking. He paused and glanced at the GI with divided attention, continuing his conversation. The young soldier stood nervously for a moment, his eyes an earnest request for attention, then he hurried back into the hallway. Several men were looking down the tracks, standing well back from the opening, peering over one another's shoulders.

One exclaimed, ''There, see, three or four, one with a machine gun.'' The Germans, in plain sight, moving into a single file about five yards apart, stooped over in a half crouch and trotted across the railroad tracks. The soldier hurriedly returned to the officer and the telephone. He spoke rapidly, ''Some more, Sir. Gosh, they are right at the Y.'' ''I can't get anything,'' the observer replied. ''They are on a fire mission.'' ''What about a cannon company?'' This from a captain. ''Not for fifteen minutes, Sir, I'll try to . . .''

He was interrupted by the chattering yammer of the 50-caliber machine gun at the end of the hallway. A pause was followed by a final, short burst of fire and the excited shouts of the gun crew. The gunner stood back in smiling elation as a companion clapped him on the shoulder, shouting, ''We got one! We got one! See!'' One German had not made it. In the dusk, his gray uniform merged with the rocks beside the tracks, his body a crumpled mound.

In the momentary quiet a GI spoke up, ''What about the men out there under the mill? They should be warned about the patrol.'' An uneasy pause, then a man, whose small stature emphasized the length of the Garand rifle barrel over his shoulder, quietly spoke up, ''That's my platoon.'' He turned instantly, clumped rapidly down the stairs, and hurried into the dark mill. The men watched him in silence.

As they again looked down the tracks there was the hiss of an incoming shell, this time from another direction, and it landed alongside of the building. Instead of an explosion it burst with a thud, a red searing core and a cloud of white smoke that filled the room and hallway with haze. "Our smoke mortar," said someone in relief, "pretty damn close, here comes another one." Two distant "spuds," long seconds in flight, burst on the other side of the house.

A GI turned his attention away from the outside to remark to Meyer and me, "you should have been here last night for pictures. Tracers were coming through the windows from every side, although I would not have wished you here. Geez, they came down the track, about a platoon, and opened fire right outside. A bazooka came right through that window and got our BAR man in the doorway. We dropped grenades on them, but they did not leave until we called in our mortars. That's why we zeroed in the phosphorus shells just now for tonight. If you fellows don't leave pretty soon you are liable to be stuck here."

"Anyone leaving who can guide us out?" Someone spoke up, "I'm going out. I'll take you, but we had better wait until this dies down."

In a lull, a half dozen of us clattered down the stairs and scuffled upon the debris along the lower hall. As we started out the door, a sudden burst of firing in the town caused us to jam up momentarily. Then in single file we trotted out across the tracks and jumped down the concrete wall under the mill.

It was dusk. The GIs at the railroad tracks behind the machine guns, their rocky barricade built up higher during the day, looked un-protected and vulnerable. Sergeant Meyer and I—alone as men branched off in various directions—followed the muddy path across the garden, through the small gate, and arrived at the house.

A few men standing along a porch next to the wall watched si-lently as Corporal Sumners joined us at the jeep. "Any shelling here?" asked Sergeant Meyer. "Not here, but they sure plastered the corner back there," replied Corporal Sumners. We climbed in and drove slowly out of the yard. It was almost dark now as we picked up speed past the derelict tank, bent low as we sped around the corner, and straightened with relief as we entered the darkness of the protective bulk of the slag pile. Sergeant Meyer turned to us, grinned, and shouted to Sumners, "Let's go Charles. I'm hungry. Chow!"

—Sergeant Ralph Butterfield

Good, Good, Complete

THE ARMY PICTORIAL SERVICE (APS) was efficiently supportive of combat cameramen. Each photographer received a critique sheet that evaluated the film he had shot. It contained not only pertinent information about exposure and focus but also technical and subject matter comments.

Pictorial continuity, an ideal of cinematography, was usually impractical to achieve in combat, where the demands of cover and limited mobility were paramount. When cameramen were aware of pictorial continuity and filmed the same subject with awareness of what the other was filming, the film editor could splice the scenes of both into an informative sequence. Sergeant Meyer describes one such instance.

Sergeant Butterfield and I, flushed with success and fresh from Fort Driant fame, turned our attention to a nondescript suburb just immediately north of the still-to-be-subjugated gray, Gothic city of Metz. Besides a ramshackle collection of Alsace architecture, Maizieres-les-Metz harbored a gigantic steel foundry, since dubbed the *Herman Goering Werke* in honor of the kinky No. 2 Nazi, but at the time in the hard-fought hands of the 90th Infantry Division.

We set our own modus operandi, recording the day-by-day advances of a single regiment assigned the task of capturing the last northern defense perimeter of Metz. We started within the battle-scarred yards of the ripped steel foundry, covering the firing of the giant 4.2 chemical mortars, which dumped even more high-arched tons of death on the *Wehrmacht*, seeking the destruction of the beleaguered Maizieres-les-Metz. An army critique of our work stated that the

material is very well covered . . . [and will be followed by] the Meyer/Butterfield team working themselves into the blasted town itself . . . getting uncomfortably close shots of the heavy, destructive mortar shells impacting well within the town's perimeter while perched precariously high on a railroad trestle alongside the most forward artillery observers.

A second critique indicated that we are getting "very good coverage showing the actual bombardment of the town with many good explosions."

Aware our coverage of the regiment's assault on Maizieres-les-Metz needed more scope, we decided to climb the very tall and very prominent gantry towers that were a structurally integral part of Herman's Steel Works. Butterfield covered the activities of the main artillery spotter in the tower closest to the town, and I held the same spotter immediately in the foreground, associating the Erector Set–like structure's relationship to the smoking target in the hazy background. On this occasion the critique was nothing short of glowing.

So why not stop when you are ahead?—not Russ and Ralph. In our qualified opinion the battalion's assault on Maizieres-les-Metz demanded an even closer peek at the town's coup de grace. Also, we couldn't help but marvel at the tenacity of the Jerries, but nobody loves a loser and a closer look is what Capt. Fred Fox got. The intrepid cameramen that we were, we found a way into the center of the ripped town, and there was certainly nothing shabby about their (the army's) final critique.

SUBJECT: MOTION PICTURE CRITIQUE

Date: *4 November 1944*

TO: *Cameramen S/Sgt. R. Butterfield*
      S/Sgt. R. Meyer
      166th Signal Photographic Co.

Unit: #NR 1

Ref: *Maizieres Les Metz, France*
      LIB. 378

Date of photography
30 Oct. 1944

Caption Sheet	*good*
Focus	*good*
Exposure	*good*
Camera Steadiness	*good*
Composition	*good*
Coverage	*good* ** complete*

COMMENTS:

**Material shows very well the terrific destruction of this town. This will tie in with previous coverage shot on the same subject.

There is very good co-ordination between cameramen.

F. F. FOX
Captain, Signal Corps

—Sergeant Russ Meyer

Wasser . . . Wasser

FOR THE GERMANS, the slag piles, steel mill, and stone houses of Maizieres-les-Metz provided formidable defense advantages. In weeks of ferocious combat with explosives, flame throwers, and ultimately hand-to-hand fighting, American infantrymen gradually pushed the defenders back. The city hall, the Hôtel de Ville, was the location of bitter fighting. At close range, a 155mm cannon blasted holes in the walls, through which GIs crawled, only to be wounded or killed in the close quarters. The hotel held out until the last day.

Behind a rolling artillery barrage, on October 29, attacking from both north and south, five companies of the 90th Division pounded the defenders, some into surrender, and the remainder into withdrawal from the battered town.

The last Germans were cleared out of Maizieres-les-Metz by October 30, and that morning Sergeant Meyer and I accompanied a few soldiers and officers into the town. A narrow, cobblestoned street led into the town square. It was omniously quiet with the strange lull of combat cessation.

A GI who had fought the night before stood in a doorway of a stone house beside the street. He looked grimy, dusty, and alert as the men passed him. He ignored the body of a German soldier a dozen yards away. The wooden door frame he leaned against was splintered and gashed. The coloration, a bright contrast to the aged wood around it, prompted a question from me.

"How did the door frame get so chewed up?" The GI moved his shoulder away from the doorway, walked a few steps into the street to observe the condition, and replied, "This house was our CP [command post] yesterday. We used that house, too." He gestured to the doorway of the house behind us, across the street, and continued, "We ran back and forth a lot. The Jerries would try and get us with rifle fire. We ran like the devil, and they would fire at the doorway, hoping to nail us there. They got the door frame plenty, but none of us." He shrugged, eyed the camera without comment, and went inside.

We walked on into the town square—an expanse with buildings on four sides, windowless and gutted. The two-storied wooden barracks had collapsed into a pile of twisted timber. An officer stood beside it and spoke downward toward the wreckage. From deep within the rubble came the faint sound of a German soldier imprisoned within. "Wasser . . . Wasser," he repeated continually. The sound of his voice indicated that he was buried deeply beneath the timbers. "Help is on the way," called the officer, and repeated his encouragement as the voice within continued the plaintive cry.

Sergeant Meyer went across the square and I remained in the

street talking to GIs. There was a small explosion from within the square, where men had been walking about, and almost immediately came the cry "Medic!" Medic!" Within minutes two medics came running down the street, a collapsed stretcher beween them. In a few minutes they returned, trotting in front and behind the stretcher. The legs and torso of the GI upon it were terribly mangled.

I joined Sergeant Meyer, who spoke heatedly, "Did you see that? The poor guy stepped on a mine. The bastards have mined the place. It happened right over there."

We filmed the destruction on the stone buildings. The structures had received puncturing damage. Huge, gaping holes had been torn out of the fronts, corners were knocked off, roofs were torn out in huge sections or blown off completely. Behind the buildings the dark bulk of the steel mill was an impersonal complement to the wreckage. Completing our filming, we paused at the wreckage of the barracks and listened. There was silence.

The battle for Maizieres-les-Metz had lasted for almost thirty days. It ended on a quiet morning with a faint cry for "Water . . . Water" from a German buried beneath wreckage and with the sharp explosion of a mine that terribly mangled an American soldier. The victory was a tribute to the persistent courage of the men of the 2nd and 3rd Battalions of the 357th Regiment, which lost over fifty-five men in the ferocious combat.

—Sergeant Ralph Butterfield

Amerika, America!

WHILE MILLIONS were being transported to Eastern Europe as victims of the Holocaust, a few thousand traveled to the West. By good fortune they escaped from the terror in Germany and found refuge in neutral countries. One young German refugee, Arthur H. Herz, after brief Americanization, enlisted in the army and distinguished himself as one of Patton's photographers.

I was born in Berlin in 1921, and was partly educated there but left Germany on account of the increasing difficulties for young Jews. With my parents I went to Italy. I worked in Florence but also found time to study at the university there. However, after half a year had passed, we were forced to leave that country too. Following a comparatively short sojourn in Switzerland and England, where my elder brother was living, my parents and I went to Cuba. In 1929 I came to Rochester, New York, to study photography at the Rochester Athenaeum and Mechanics Institute.

These studies coincided with the outbreak of World War II but were not greatly influenced by those cataclysmic events. Indeed, I was turned down in my attempts to enlist in the Canadian Active Service; I still have the 1940 letter from the Department of National Defense in Ottawa, wherein it is politely pointed out that for reasons of nationality, I was ineligible to fight on the Allied side.

The same attitude was displayed in Rochester's navy recruitment office, where on Monday morning, December 8, 1941, I presented myself as a healthy, willing, and eager youngster. In fact, it was not until a year later, after I had graduated in Photographic Technology at Mechanics Institute and had worked for a month as a laboratory technician in Eastman Kodak's research laboratory, that the United States Army relented and accepted me. My military qualifications consisted of excellent health, a strong body, good education and training, and the will to do everything in my power to help win the war for the Allies and the world. More than most soldiers, I knew what the war was all about!

Following basic training at Camp Croft, Spartenburg, South Carolina—where I was taken off guard duty to be sworn in as a U.S. citizen—I volunteered for the parachute troops. However, the army had different plans. Instead of jump training I was posted in the spring of 1943 to the 166th Signal Photo Company at Camp Crowder, Missouri. There is nothing interesting to report about my stateside duties except that I contracted pneumonia during maneuvers in Tennessee and had to be hospitalized in Nashville. As a result, the 166th shipped to Europe without me and it was not until Christmas Day, 1944, in Metz, France, that I again managed to join up with elements of that company.

To be more precise, at that time in Metz, I became a member of Lt. Adrien Salvas's photo detachment, which was part of the 35th Division, Third United States Army, and was making its way out of Metz to go into the Ardennes and join the Battle of the Bulge. That detachment, which included as my steady companion motion picture cameraman Sgt. Barney Caliendo, was shifted occasionally to other divisions and even to different armies. Thus, at one time, I participated in actions of Montgomery's Twenty-first Army Group in Holland, and somewhat later I found myself attached to the United States Seventh Army into the south near the Vosges Mountains. However, I stayed with the same detachment through V-E Day and eventual demobilization.

Much of a divisional photographer's activities in the European theater of operations was centered on obtaining pictures for record and publicity purposes. Generally, our troops welcomed the presence of cameramen. Most of the soliders liked the idea of having their action recorded, maybe even published in *Stars and Stripes* or in their hometown newspaper. Hence, the caption sheets that accompanied the film packs to the processing laboratory in the rear often contained simple, illustrated stories. In the recurring theme of war and peace, I remember that I often attempted to show pictorially and describe in the caption the incongruity of battle and its aftermath: for example, wounded men being treated in a battalion aid station in a crypt decorated with trumpet-blowing angels; a dead soldier in a burned-out tank with a church in the background; a little girl cradling a kitten in the smoking ruins of her farm.

Sometimes the caption sheets described more general activity of the infantry which was witnessed by the cameraman. This is illustrated by example dated March 26, 1945.

Det. 4, 166th Signal Photo Co.
89th Inf. Div.
3rd U.S. Army
APO - 89

March 26th, 45

Super XX Packs

Cameraman: T/5 A. H. Herz

Master C A P T I O N

At 2 o'clock in the morning elements of the 353 Inf. Regt. 89th Div. left their side of the Rhine at Oberwesel to assault the German positions at the right side of the river.

It was not until 6:30 A.M. that the light was sufficient for picture taking.

The road that parallels the river and from which the engineers and infantry launched their storm boats was partially concealed by the artificial smoke laid by a Negro Chem. Warfare unit. The gutter and ditch of the road is choked with inf. men who seek protection and cover from MG bullets and mortar fire that the Heinies keep throwing from the other side. A particularly deep ditch or underpass serves as a BN. CP.

Ducks of the 354 A.T.C. rumble up the road to take on a load of scrambling inf. men who have to leave the scant cover of road and ditch for the lofty but exposed height of the Duck. It takes them over a few rails and a small bridge to the bank of the Rhine; with a splash it rolls in and swims on.

Crouching low for maximum concealment, the inf. men's faces register many varying emotions as the bullets whizz by and mortar shells throw up fountains of water. Once on the other side of the Rhine the men drop off fast to form their lines.

Upon crossing to the Oberwesel side, the Ducks take on Jerry PWs some of whom are wounded, there are also two or three Volkssturm characters. After reaching land the PWs give first aid to their wounded while infantry reinforcements move past through the smoke to board the Ducks that are waiting for them.

All the houses and villages that form the background of

some of the pictures are part of Oberwesel; the castle on the hill is Schloss Schoenburg belonging to the Rhinelander Family of New York City.

N O T E

The artificial fog, poor light and rain as well as a busted rangefinder made for very unsatisfactory photographic conditions. Continued duplication shots seemed the only answer to assure adequate coverage.

Because of necessary underexposure, *ADD DEVLOP. TIME.*

Actually, some of the photographs turned out reasonably well and were nicely recognized by inclusion in 1950 in the *Time* publication "Life's Picture History of World War II," and by the military, as illustrated by the following.

COMPANY "A"
3908th SIGNAL SERVICE BATTALION (GHQ PICTORIAL)
UNITED KINGDOM BASE, ETO.
APO, 413. U S ARMY

FFO/le.
4 April 1945

SUBJECT: Commendation.

TO   : Commanding Officer, 3908 Signal Service Battn (GHQ Pictorial) APO. 887 U S Army. Att. Maj. H. W. McAllistar, OIC. Still Picture Operations.

1. It is desired to commend Tec 5 A. H. Herz, Detachment 4, 166th Signal Photo Co. for his coverage of a recent assignment.

2. Tec 5 Herz accompanied elements of the 89th Infantry Division during their crossing of the Rhine and assault on the German city of Oberwesel on 26 March. His negatives were exposed under extreme conditions of artificial fog, poor light, and rain, in addition to the fact that his range finder was not functioning.

3. Despite handicaps mentioned above, coverage of the assignment was superior from every standpoint, and the resulting prints (ETO HQ 45-23733-23546, inclusive) rank among the best action pictures made in this Theatre.

4. It is requested that a copy of this letter be forwarded through channels to the photographer involved.

FRANK F. ORR
1st Lt. Signals Corps.
OIC News Section

Just the same, it often seemed to me that the major contribution I made during the European campaign was based upon my fluent knowledge of German. My background and this knowledge facilitated the rapid location of specific sites in a town we were trying to overrun, the evaluation of captured documents, and the interrogation of PWs. In fact, to be able to holler into a bunker "Kommt raus, der Krieg ist for euch vorbei!" made it possible for me to collect a particularly large number of prisoners who were ready to give up and only needed the reassurance of familiar words; though this desire to talk Germans into giving up the fight was an invitation that was sometimes not received with raised hands but with a few rounds from a burp gun.

Having mentioned some advantages due to my fluency in German, I should also indicate that my native tongue occasionally got me into deep and almost grievous trouble. As my children will have little difficulty believing even today, in the mid-1940s I spoke with a rather guttural German accent; clearly Pvt. Arthur Herz was not a native New England Yankee! This circumstance caused little trouble until late in 1944 when I attempted to transfer from the 583rd Signal Depot Company to rejoin the 166th Signal Photo Company. When approval was finally received, it seemed a simple matter to take my transfer orders and gear (including some "confiscated" fancy United States Army signal equipment) and hitch a ride to nearby units of the photo company.

The trouble was the date: December 16, 1944. At the very time that I set off from a village in Luxembourg as a passenger in a supply truck, Von Rundstedt's armies also set off on their last offense. I found that out when our truck encountered heavy traffic of obviously disorganized (that is a euphemism) motorized equipment going helter-skelter in the opposite direction. At some crossroads near Echternach, we learned that the Germans had broken through our lines. While the driver decided not to endanger his cargo and returned to the rear, I determined to leave the truck at this road intersection and asked for directions to my old outfit.

The place was then beginning to come under fire, and I had a chance to ask questions or directions for troop locations only once before being jumped by our soldiers with guns at the ready. I was quickly disarmed and searched. Apparently reports of German parachutists in American uniforms had come and the evidence against me seemed overwhelming: I didn't have a password; I didn't understand baseball scores; and in a suspiciously un-American manner I did not know who had won the pennant. Moreover, in a most unarmy-like fashion, I carried my own transfer papers together with some new-fangled signal equipment. All of that plus my music hall German accent was too much for the MP sergeant, who took charge of "the Kraut bastard in a GI uniform who wants us to believe that he comes from Upstate New York." The noise and confusion from the nearby fighting which was going badly for us put me in imminent danger of conviction and execution by the nervous MP, who had to be convinced that there was more glory for him in receiving a medal for uncommon vigilance in apprehending a cleverly disguised bona fide German spy than by shooting a man in a GI uniform whose accent and treacherous activity could then not verified.[1]

Apparently the point was well made: I was carted away to Liege with some other Heinies as a special PW. Following some further unpleasantness, when it was uncertain whether I would be finished off by my former or by my present compatriots, I was released nine days later on Christmas Day in Metz. Thus I was again on the right side of the United States Army and found myself participating as already mentioned in the Battle of the Bulge, the Rhine crossing, and the victorious push into Germany up the Isar in Bavaria.

It was there, while attempting to cover the Isar River crossing near Landshut, that I endeavored to persuade Germans to surrender. They responded with shots. A slug in the side ended the war for me, just about a week before V-E Day.

—Sergeant Arthur H. Herz

---

[1]Hitler directed Col. Otto Skorzeny to form a special brigade of German troops wearing American uniforms and with the ability to speak Americanized English. They were to penetrate into American territory with jeeps, seize bridges and disrupt communications. Eighteen were captured, wearing German uniforms beneath American, and were summarily shot. Charles B. MacDonald, *A Time For Trumpets,* pp. 15, 226.

Sgt. Arthur Herz

"CROUCHING LOW for maximum concealment, the inf.[antry] men's faces register many varying emotions as the bullets whizz by and mortar shells throw up fountains of water. Once on the other side of the Rhine the men drop off fast to form their lines."

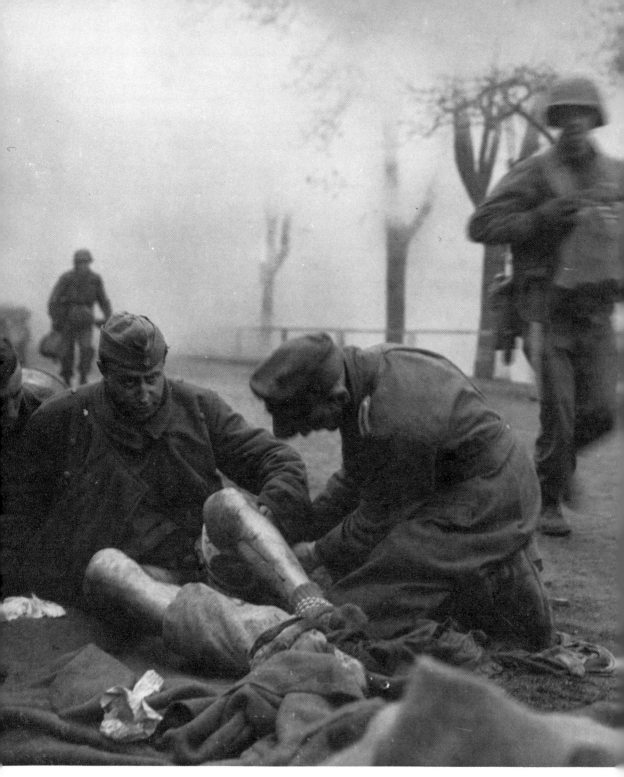

Sgt. Arthur He

"UPON CROSSING to the Oberwesel side, the Duck takes on Jerry PWs, some of whom are wounded; there are also two or three Volkssturm characters. After reaching land the PWs give first aid to their wounded while infantry reinforcements move past through the smoke to board the Ducks that are waiting for them."

Sgt. Arthur Herz

"DUCKS OF THE 354 A.T.C. rumble up the road to take on a load of scrambling inf.[antry] men who have to leave the scant cover of road and ditch for the lofty but exposed height of the Duck."

Sgt. Arthur He

THE MOMENT of a German soldier's decision to surrender was frequently one of suspense. There was always the possibility of error in communication or fatal trickery. Upon orders this German tossed weapons out of the window; thereupon, he and his companions came out with their hands raised.

Lt. Adrien Salvas

PRISONERS WERE REQUIRED to supply only name, rank, and serial number. In practice they voluntarily provided much additional information about the numerical strength, unit identification, and placement of their troops.

The Conquistador

ARMY COMMAND frequently encouraged initiative and self-reliance by enlisted men. There was a fine line between regimented discipline and individuality. It was a distinctive influence of a free society upon military tradition. Men who posssessed drive and purpose sometimes found oportunity to utilize these traits.

Warren was sitting on top of the truck, his heels banging against the side, and I sat in the open front seat beside Harry, who was driving with his usual aplomb. He drove the three-quarter-ton truck as though it was his personal sports car, beeping the horn with a sideward flourish of first one hand and then the other at the sluggish morning traffic in Pilsen. For the bicyclists he used a special, gleeful blast, and Czech workmen found themselves with a sporting chance to waver between truck and curbing. At an intersection a policeman waved us through, stopping the side traffic, his white club held chest high, rigidly parallel with the ground.

In the confinement between the buildings the air was smelly with the exhaust fumes from charcoal burning trucks, the smoke becoming a blue haze that softened the stark brown tones of the old buildings. The cobblestones joggled us comfortably, rattling our camera equipment inside the metal panels of the truck. Harry had taken the truck into Third Army headquarters at Bad Tölz in Germany, and they had built an aluminum body from captured German metals. It had a door in the back, with a ladder to the top, which was flat and strong enough to support the weight of the heavy sound camera while the truck was in motion. Warren, the sound technician, swung himself with agile assurance down the ladder and inside the truck. He pounded a mattress into position for comfortable reclining and laid down with one foot hooked around a ladder step.

The street led into the suburbs, past the lounging MPs in front of the Pilsen brewery and up a hill. The truck climbed slowly, the low gears humming and grinding. The Berounka curved through the city below us, sparkling as the haze lifted under the warmth of the sun, and the red tile roofs dotted the view in a lovely pattern. Over the top the road wound through the orderly Czech country. The rolling hills were covered with pine forests, interspersed with valleys of farmlands. In the villages most of the houses had the red, white, and blue Czech flag hanging in celebration of the liberation, for it was only a few weeks earlier in this spring of May 1945 that Czechoslovakia had been freed from German occupation.

Children waved and shouted as we drove along, and Harry yelled for Warren to give him some candy from inside the truck. Warren, with annoyed impatience, slowly poked among the boxes and passed some glassine-wrapped hard candies through the window. Harry threw them at the youngsters, enjoying the ensuing scrambling as much as he had the same antics of French children in Normandy eleven months earlier. He lived with dramatic flair in his role as a newsreel photographer, and dangerous experiences as a combat cameraman before his recent promotion to the sound unit had not detracted from his personal image of liberating benefactor.

Adults waved to us with great enthusiasm, for they saw a dearth of Allied trucks along the road. It led to Prague, the capital of Czechoslovakia, which was occupied by the Russian army. By political arrangement Russian forces occupied most of the fifty-five miles between Pilsen and Prague. There was no friendly, unofficial visiting between the two zones. The Russians who inadvertently, or purposely, motored into the American zone were taken into custody. They were questioned and escorted back to the line of demarcation—a neutral zone a mile wide.

It was to this we were traveling, three sergeant photographers from the Third Army photographic company. Harry had learned that President Benes was returning from exile to Prague and, impatient with headquarters life, had requested permission to film the arrival of Benes in the capital. His commanding officer gave him verbal permission to do so. At Fifth Corps headquarters he asked me to go along and help with the hand-held Eymo camera, although it was as much to drive the lumbering truck that I was needed. My signal officer gave me the same gratuitous permission, with the assurance that it was impossible. The Russians would not let anyone through. Expecting to be back for supper, we loaded with a week's supply of film, gasoline, and ten-in-one rations.

In the midst of a dense grove of trees, about ten miles from Pilsen, we came upon a dozen people loitering beside the road. A little way beyond them a group of Russian soldiers stood around a tank that was facing in our direction, its gun commanding the highway. As we approached, a Russian soldier walked to the center of the road and vigorously waved a red flag up and down. As Harry stopped next to him another one strolled over to my side, and both watched us with casual disinterest. They gave no sign of understanding as Harry explained first in English, then in French, what we desired. The one on his side responded by waving his hand imperiously toward the side of the road. Harry repeated his story, less politely and more demandingly, and again he was interrupted by the emphatic hand, signaling us off the road.

The confident self-assertiveness of being liberator-conqueror for nearly a year would not be discouraged by rebuff, and Harry took matters into his own hands. Pointing confidently down the road, and putting the truck in gear, he started out. The expressions of both guards changed from impassiveness to angry scowls as they jumped onto the running board of the truck. The weapon of one slipped off his shoulder, cracking me on the knee, and clattered against the fender. The other grabbed the steering wheel, then twisted his machine pistol around so it pointed at Harry's midriff. He jammed on the brakes, which projected both guards running upon the ground. They both whirled around and pointed their weapons at us. The motionless tension was broken by Warren's sarcastic voice from the window, "I think he means STOP, Harry."

Harry pulled the truck over under the trees, and for a moment we sat wordlessly, recovering our composure. Then Harry suggested we try an officer, and we walked to one standing near the tank. He was dressed in a black uniform and was tall and slender in contrast to the short stature of the soldiers. He listened to us politely, his facial expression responsive and intelligent as we showed him our SHAEF correspondent's pass. It was printed in English and French and requested that military commanders extend the bearer cooperation in photographing all military operations. He examined it methodically as we talked in English, halting French, and the German I remembered from college. We assured him that Generals Eisenhower, Bradley, and Patton were all deeply interested in the vital importance of our mission—desperately hoping that such free and easy name dropping would bridge our gap. He responded by courteously handing the SHAEF pass back to us, turning his back, and walking off.

We returned to our truck in disappointment, where Warren, who took a dim view of the whole expedition, tartly suggested that we go back before the Russians decided to take a more unfriendly interest in us. We decided to have lunch first and sat on the ground under a tree with our ten-in-one ration box before us. We watched the Russians interrogate a busload of passengers from Prague. While two officers checked identification, others gave the luggage a perfunctory examination. Said Harry to Warren, "How would you like that every time you left Pennsylvania?" Not to be moved from his disapproval Warren munched in silence, torn between eating his candy or giving it to the small boy who stood before him with eyes expressing a yearning his lips would not.

A black sedan arrived from the Russian zone. It parked near the tank, where several guards gathered around it. The officer we had accosted suddenly left the group, came over to us, and held out his hand. I gave him my SHAEF pass and he returned to the car with it. "I hope you see it again," was Warren's ironic comment.

In a few minutes he returned and handed me the pass, with a small piece of notepaper inserted inside of it. It was about two-by-six inches, and on it was written two lines in Russian. He nodded to us and gestured with his hand down the road toward Prague. With surprised, elated glances at one another, we threw our boxes hastily into the truck.

"Let's go before they change their minds," commented Harry as he drove the truck to the two guards and handed one the piece of paper. The guard read it slowly, returned it, stepped back, and waved his flag for us to proceed. Hardly believing our luck, we drove past the tank, the bus, the other guards, and into the Russian zone. We sat rigidly for a hundred yards as the truck picked up speed. Harry turned in triumph to Warren and shouted, "Well, Warren?" Warren's return was an exuberant yell as he glanced back at the roadblock disappearing behind us.

We finished our lunch as we drove through pleasant Bohemia, the road leading through forests and small villages, over streams, and past clean farm buildings. In a narrow section the road curved back and forth, and as we rounded a bend Harry slammed on the brakes. The road ahead was blocked, the way congested with an approaching Russian convoy of trucks and tanks. We slowed to a crawl, squeezing along the right shoulder of the road, past the first dozen vehicles, well into the convoy. The passage became narrow as larger trucks blocked the way, until we were jammed in too tightly to go forward, or to back out.

Glancing uneasily at one another, we waited for someone to challenge us, as the ever-optimistic Warren called out to have our pass ready. Nothing happened. Russian soldiers stood by their trucks, others walked about talking and smoking. We silently appraised them and received only the casual detached scrutiny that we had gotten from the guards at the line of demarcation. We got out, stretched our legs, and looked at the tanks and equipment. Many drivers were tinkering with the engines, accelerating them to a clattering crescendo, black clouds of exhaust smoke spewing from the backs. The vehicles were a wide assortment of captured German army makes and sizes, with white stars painted over the *Wehrmacht* tan. The majority of them were in poor condition.

We separated momentarily as our curiosity led us along the line. As I was peering at the running gear of a tank I felt a firm tap on my shoulder. Bracing myself for an awkward explanation, I turned and found myself confronted with a small, middle-aged soldier. His legs were slightly bowed, his face wrinkled and tanned. Indicating the camera around my neck, he pointed to a black sedan coming toward us, twisting and turning its way between the trucks. He gestured forcibly toward the car, repeating "General Gordov" several times. His tone and gesture implied that anything less than a photograph would be discourteous, and I hastily unslung my camera. Holding it to my eye I framed and focused rapidly. Ten months of experience were summoned at this delicate moment, and I snapped the shutter in time to get an excellent picture—of the door handle sweeping by the lens. He nodded in approval, looking enviously at the camera, and I rapidly snapped the case around it before his envy changed to desire.

I offered him a cigarette. He lit up, inhaled, and looked at the smoke with real appreciation. Quickly pulling a pack out of his pocket, he offered me one, pushing the pack toward me insistently when I hesitated. The cigarettes were mangled and ill formed, with shreds of coarse stubble sticking out of the ends. With misgivings I too lit up, inhaled tentatively, and struggled to conceal my distaste for the acrid combination of unpleasant flavors. Puffing away with blissful satisfaction, my companion was nearly at the end of his smoke. Looking reflectively at the butt, he suddenly pulled the package out of his pocket, insisted that I accept it, then waited expectantly. I slowly offered him my full pack, which he grabbed. Nodding his thanks he abruptly walked away, lighting a new cigarette from the butt of the old.

Behind me came the faint sound of shouted orders, and truck engines started with a cacophony of sounds; the slow "chug chug" of the diesels mingled with the clattering rattle of gasoline engines. As the convoy moved slowly we boarded and cautiously traveled in the opposite direction—the vehicles making way for us to squeeze through.

A ditch paralleled the road on our side, and beyond it was an embankment ten feet high. Upon it two attractive teenage girls, both carrying heavily loaded handbags, were being questioned by several Russians. A young officer held an identification card in his hand, and his teasing interrogation was amusing to his friends and embarrassing to the blushing girls. Glancing below to include the convoy soldiers in his audience brought us to his attention. Looking us over keenly he handed the card to one of the girls, ran down the embankment, jumped the ditch, hopped on the running board, and half-seated himself beside me.

Holding on to the windshield with one hand he turned to me, and in a confident, appraising tone said, "English?" I shook my head, and he continued, "American?" When I nodded he asked in German if I understood the language. "Somewhatly," I replied, and he thought intently. Then in German, forming his sentence with confidence and pronouncing the words with unhesitating assurance, he declared, "I am very sorry that President Roosevelt is dead; he was a great, good man." He nodded in completion, and hardly waited for my "Danke Schön" he jumped down and recrossed the ditch. As I recovered from my surprise, and translated for the others, with one accord we looked behind. The blushing girls, their eyes averted, were again an unwilling supporting role to his performance upon the embankment.

The road led upward and downward as the country became hillier. We started down one slope, and on the upgrade ahead a car was stalled. Two civilians were plumbing the gas tank with a stick, and the third waved frantically as we approached. Harry slowed, looked them over carefully, and stopped behind the car.

The young man who flagged us was clean-cut in appearance, and with courteous eagerness he said, "Pardon, could you help us with a little petrol, enough to carry us to Prague? Are you English, perhaps?" "We are Americans, how much farther . . ." Harry was interrupted by the Czech, who with great excitement exclaimed, "Americans!" The Americans are coming, yes? You are the first, perhaps, of many troops?" "No, we are by ourselves," replied Harry. "But I do not understand how you are here, you have a special mission, perhaps that you travel alone to Prague? I am very disappointed that other Americans are not coming too. Can you tell me why American army does not come to Prague also?" "We do not know that," said Harry. "Let's put some gas in your car." We poured about a gallon in their tank and learned that the name of the young man was Fred and that he lived in an apartment with his mother in the city.

Harry invited him to ride with us, and as we conversed he told Fred of our plans. Fred immediately insisted that we stay in his apartment. Our truck could be parked off the street in a garage, the manager of which was his friend. He suggested with whom we might start to make arrangements for photography and guided us to the offices. He lived near the center of the city, in convenient proximity to the locales of public events.

While we talked over our arrangements with him, our road reached the suburbs of Prague and Fred directed us through it along a street leading to a broad, beautiful river in the middle of the city. The bridge across it was partially blocked by a barricade of cobblestones, topped with coils of barbed wire. Workmen were returning the square pieces of granite to the road, laying them in a bed of sand, snugly fitting them together without mortar between the joints.

"Was there much fighting in the city?" I asked Fred. "Yes," he replied, "there was very bitter fighting between the Germans and the Russians. Many of the Czech partisans were killed fighting the Germans. The Germans set fire to the town hall, it is very old, fifteenth century. Many homes were damaged in the residential district of Pankrac, where the fighting was most intense."

As we passed over the middle of the river many other bridges came into view, upstream and down, gracefully linking the banks of the city. Behind us, downstream to our left, a tremendous group of regal buildings crested a wooded, green hill. The spacious, many-storied bulk of the one facing the river was surmounted by the spires of a cathedral behind it, whose slender towers flecked the sky. In the wooded slopes falling sharply to the river glinted red tile roofs and narrow streets twisted down the slope through the trees.

"What's that layout up there?" asked Harry, motioning over his shoulder. "Layout?" was Fred's puzzled reply. "Those buildings?" "Oh," continued Fred, "that is the seat of the Czech government, Prague Castle. We call it Hradcany Castle. It was the residence of the kings of Bohemia as well as the president of the Czechoslovak Republic from 1918 to 1938. It will be the capitol of our government when President Benes returns again. Behind it is the Saint Vitus Cathedral."

It looked extremely imposing—and impenetrable. Admittance would seem to require more influence and credentials than our prima facie represented. I glanced at Harry, and reading my unspoken thoughts he exclaimed with his usual élan, "That's where we will be in a few days, eh, Warren!" Warren appraised the beautiful buildings, dominating the river view, and responded, "We will be lucky if they let us ring the front door bell."

When we had crossed the bridge, Fred directed us, and as we followed a street along the river Harry noticed several men in British uniforms leaning against the sidewalk railing. He pulled over to the curb and called to them, "Are you English?" They trotted across the street, and as we shook hands all around they told us they were liberated New Zealand PWs waiting for transportation.

"Are you an advance party of Yanks?" asked one. When we explained our mission they readily agreed to a motion picture interview. While we set up the camera, Warren arranged his sound equipment, placing the microphone near the railing and leading the cable into the back of the truck. Fred left, saying that he would prepare his mother for the addition to their apartment.

As I interviewed the soldiers, who related some of their experiences as prisoners of the Germans, a crowd of Czechs gathered to watch. They were considerate and circumspect in their demeanor. With polite deference one said to me, "Pardon, are you English, perhaps?" I replied we were Americans, and his expression quickened in interest. With suppressed excitement he exclaimed, "You are the first of many Americans?" I regretfully informed him that we were not. As he comprehended, his eagerness died, and with reproachful, almost fatalistic sadness, he said, "We have hoped that Americans would come and occupy Prague."

He spoke slowly, struggling to express his feelings, as he continued, "We have a great liking for America, you know." The quizzical sadness of his expression left much unsaid, and I had the uncomfortable feeling that I represented something that had failed him. He returned to the curb and talked to some others, as I interviewed the next person.

As I finished, a Czech touched me on the arm, saying, "If you will pardon me, I have been told that you are Americans, is that so?" Upon my confirmation, he continued, "You are the first of many Americans who will come to Prague, perhaps?" He inflected the last word with the same half-hopeful eagerness that others had used, and his expression was crestfallen when I stated that we were alone. Then he continued, "Why do not Americans come to Prague? We are a democracy, you know. Your tanks came, and then they turned and went back." I searched my mind for a reason, and finding none could only shrug my shoulders and reply that it was for military reasons I did not understand. He stared for a moment across the river, his eyes squinting fatalistically, then turned his back and walked away down the street.

Harry, always alert to the seductive influence of the camera, motioned me toward an attractive young woman watching us from the front of the spectators. I moved over to her and asked, "Do you live here in Prague?" She hesitated momentarily, then in slightly accented English replied, "Yes, I have been here for ten years. I have been in the academy." Her intimately husky voice and balanced posture were suggestive cues to the next question, "What did you study at the academy?" She paused, glanced at Harry beside his camera, and replied, "The Academy of Dance. I am a member of the ballet of the Opera National. Please, may you attend our performance?" She hurriedly dug into her handbag and produced a card.

"Okay boys, wrap it up," said Harry, stepping forward and taking the card. He conversed busily with her as I turned to help Warren, and their conversation continued as the crowd dispersed and we stowed the equipment into the truck. She wrote on the card, smiled at Harry, and turned away.

"What a knockout," enthused Harry, card in hand, watching her walk away from us. Harry, prone to impromptu musings, added with solemn admiration, "Poetry in motion." "That's not all that's in motion," observed Warren as he pulled himself into the back of the truck.

We found Fred's apartment and the security of the truck in the garage ideal for our needs. Our acquaintanceship with Fred became a friendship. We had arrived in Prague Saturday, May 12, and the arrival of President Benes was scheduled for the following Wednesday. Monday morning we started with the first official Fred recommended. The day was spent going from office to office, conferring with bureaucrats. We were greeted with neutrality by some, shunted off by the office staff of others, and treated with enthusiastic eagerness by many. The practical results were not encouraging at first.

Harry proved to be indefatigable. His personality was enthusiastic and friendly, as he followed each lead with dogged zeal. His aggressive determination, lack of both rank and credentials, and obvious disregard for conventional channels of communication was puzzling to many officials. Their reactions made us aware that our presence in the city was unique and coalesced an awareness of our vulnerability.

Late in the afternoon we achieved our first goal—written authority to be in the parade with our truck. Arrangements for a personal interview with President Benes appeared unlikely. Harry persisted the next day, the parade pass opening doors to higher echelons of officials. He was informed that after the president arrived our request would be submitted to his staff.

After lunch, as we reloaded the cameras on the table in Fred's apartment, Harry produced the card from the woman we had met the afternoon of our arrival and handed it to Fred. "Any idea where this person lives?" Fred examined the card and exclaimed with his customary enthusiasm, "This person is a dancer in the Czech National Opera. Look! Her address is just across the street. Here, come, I will show you." They leaned out the window, and Fred pointed to windows across and down the street. We were on the third floor of a building identical with all those in the entire block, in which sheer-walled apartments crowded the narrow sidewalks below us.

Fred continued, "There, you see the windows at our level across the street, about fifty meters in that direction? Somewhere in there is the address of the apartment on this card. Where did you get this?" "Harry is looking for a shack-up," said Warren. "We got it from a girl we interviewed." "Shack-up?" said Fred in puzzlement. "I do not understand." "Harry is very successful with amour," I added.

"Ah, the conquering lover," exclaimed Fred with a burst of laughter. "The conquistador with the yellow scarf." A language professor, he looked at Harry with keen interest. Harry did not respond. He was in front of a mirror combing his hair and adjusting the knot of the yellow silk parachute remnant that he wore tied around his neck. Months before he had cut it from one of the discarded chutes available in Normandy.

"Back in about an hour," he remarked as he went out the door. "Be sure the equipment is ready to go; we will do some filming around the city this afternoon."

I cleaned the film gate of the Eymo camera and labeled some film cans. Fred's mother joined us, and he translated many questions that she asked about America. In a little over an hour we were interrupted by a familiar shout, "WARREN!" It was a bellow, from outside the window, down the street. "WARREN!" Harry had a powerful voice, and he frequently annoyed Warren with his shouted commands. We leaned out the window, Warren's expression one of pained annoyance. The street was vacant of traffic.

Harry was seated on a window ledge about forty yards from us, legs inside the room, his upper body outside the building, holding on with one hand, shirtless, his hair in disarray, the yellow ribbon fluttering as he shouted, "GET THE TRUCK!" His booming voice, bouncing between the flat walls of the buildings, was amplified by the reverberations. "GET THE TRUCK. I'LL BE THERE IN A FEW MINUTES!" He pulled himself inside and disappeared. We ducked our heads back into the room, and discovered Fred at our elbows, an astonished witness to the novel communication. With a look of incredulity he commented, "Harry is like the cowboy in the films of the old west. He always gets the beautiful maiden." "One way or another," agreed Warren.

Wednesday morning was warm and brilliantly sunny as we drove to the Woodrow Wilson Railroad Station. We had loaded our cameras before starting. Harry had mounted his tripod on the roof, chaining it down snugly while Warren fastened a sign lettered *FILM* on the front of the truck.

An atmosphere of expectant, holiday gaiety prevailed along the sidewalks as people moved briskly toward the parade streets. The dark clothing of the men was a foil for the colorful blouses and skirts of the women dressed in Czech national costume. Huge red banners that had a yellow hammer and sickle in the top right corner were fastened to the third stories of many buildings—the ten-foot widths cascading down in impressive billows to where they were fastened above the street doors.

We turned at Hoover Boulevard and arrived at the station. The cleared street in front was guarded by Russian soldiers, spaced five yards apart, their backs to the throngs of people jamming the sidewalk. Harry steered to a position guarded by Czechs and showed them the pass he had received the morning before. An official read it with businesslike impatience, which changed to excited interest as he beckoned us through. He shook Harry's hand vigorously as he handed back the paper.

Harry drove into the cleared space, and with an appraising survey of the lineup of official cars in front of the station entrance, wheeled the truck around and parked it near the middle of the street. The position would enable him to photograph downward upon the red carpet leading from the station doorway to the front limousine. It also placed us in conspicuous isolation in the middle of the clearing, the subject of interest for hundreds of people.

We got out and busily set up the equipment. Harry lifted his heavy sound camera to the top, fastened it to the tripod head, and connected the sound cable to it as Warren handed it up from inside. A civilian approached us and speaking in English suggestive of years of residence in America introduced himself as Mr. Sima, our guide and translator. He answered our friendly questions about his life in America with noncommittal reserve, nonconducive to prolonged conversation.

As Harry locked the film magazine into place two Russian soldiers walked toward us. I examined a front tire, covertly watching them, and inside I could see Warren keeping them in view as he worked on his equipment. As they stopped beside the truck to watch Harry, one turned his back partially toward me. Clipped to his belt hung an Eymo camera, similar to my army issue. Hurriedly pulling mine out of its case, I walked over and offered it for his perusal. He pulled his around and we compared them, discovering that his was manufactured in America and identical with mine. Mine had an improved winding handle, which one pointed out to the other, and they looked it over with professional interest. Two others joined us, colleagues of the first pair, and by unspoken cordiality we recognized our mutual status.

When one climbed a few rungs of the ladder to get a close look at the sound camera, Harry beckoned to him vigorously, booming, "Come on up!" He racked the camera back and forth, adjusted the viewfinder so the Russian could look through it, and pointed out the threading of the film. One of the Russians made himself comfortable checking his own camera. The officer in charge of the photographers offered a friendly grin. With Mr. Sima translating he showed me his card, which identified him as Captain Monflein, director of a documentary film organization in Moscow. I told him about our film transportation to the States and tried to elicit conversation of common interest. He was noncommittal about factual information but remained friendly and cordial. He accompanied me as I walked about taking pictures of the people in the crowd.

Many young people were in uniform, the Communists in green with large yellow stars on garrison caps. The Boy Scouts wore tan uniforms with merit badges and caps identical with our American ones. When I filmed the women in beautifully beaded, starched national costume, Captain Monflein beckoned me to a particularly lovely girl in an elaborate, ruffled bodice, with high leg-of-mutton sleeves. Her headpiece was a foot high, of variegated flowers, framing the translucent delicacy of her complexion and the brilliant blue of her eyes. As we walked on I pointed to the only woman officer in the vicinity—a tall girl in a white beret. Leading me to the retinue of officers who surrounded her, he made the request, and upon her acquiescence she watched the camera as it ran—her expression one of unsmiling composure.

The leisurely walk of the officials in and out of the station changed into a tempo of rapid movements and intense consultations. The crowd sensing that the train had arrived made the doorway the focus of expectations. As the passage was cleared for the limousine and an entourage filled the station entrance from within, there was an expectant quiet.

President Benes walked slowly from the dark entrance of the station, pausing momentarily in the brilliant sunlight. His small stature was resolute in bearing, his expression that of sober intentness. Mrs. Benes accompanied him, wearing beautifully styled clothing and moving with graciousness and poise. A roar of shouting greeted him, to the accompaniment of riotous waving of small flags and flowers. "Nazdar," a word of enthusiastic acclaim, was repeated with increasing fervor. He raised his hand in acknowledgment, then slowly escorted Mrs. Benes into the roofless car, where he paused again, standing up in the rear compartment and gesturing to his tanks in the crowd—his face unsmiling.

Rewinding my camera, I ran to our truck where Captain Monflein waited on the running board. As I climbed over the spare tire into the driver's seat he gestured an offer to take pictures with my camera. As I handed it to him and started the engine, a Czech policeman jumped onto the running board beside me and without warning pummeled my left arm with his fist, shouting, "STOP, STOP!"

As I looked at him in surprise, Harry's yells from above reached me, "GO, GO!" "Stop?" I sputtered, then yelled, "What do you mean stop, we have not even started yet!" His response was to flay my arm violently, shouting "Stop!" with each blow of his fist. Pulling ahead in low gear I sought to peer around him and keep our truck even with the president's car. This moved the policeman's violence to hysteria. He pounded with both hands as the president's car accelerated ahead of us.

As the limousine pulled ahead Harry bawled from above, "FASTER, FASTER!" and "STOP, STOP!" from beside me. Shifting into second gear I lurched the truck forward, hoping to lose my tormentor. He clutched the windshield with one hand, pulling me with the other arm. Struggling to keep the truck from swerving I accelerated, the truck shaking unmercifully over the cobblestones. As his camera vibrated, Harry's yells changed to shrieks, "SLOW UP, SLOW UP!"

A glance over my shoulder revealed him hugging the camera and tripod in frantic desperation. As we abruptly slackened speed the policeman was thrown forward. He wavered uncertainly, then desperately grabbed my left arm with both hands. His weight inexorably pulled the steering wheel over and we slowly entered the line of cars in the procession, gradually taking our place in the parade. Harry was filming once again, and the policeman seemed mollified with our position as the parade progressed.

Along the street people jammed the sides from curbs to buildings, the sunlight glittering in giddy movement upon thousands of arms waving flags and pictures of President Benes. For the next half hour the tremendous sound of "Nazdar" assailed us in overpowering intensity, the tremendous roar creating an unnerving sensation of physical pressure.

We turned into broad Wenceslas Avenue, the people solidly filling the six lanes, leaving a narrow way down one side for the parade. Ahead of us was a jeep-load of Russian officers, which followed a rear-engined Skoda car. The procession turned to the right along the river at the end of the avenue, followed Masaryk Avenue to the Charles Bridge, and then turned right into the city. The route was lined with cheering spectators. Russian soldiers were on both sides of the streets, spaced about ten yards apart, with their backs to the people and their weapons at "Present Arms."

We emerged into Old Town Square, and as the vehicles ahead of us turned into side streets, I drove straight ahead. The crowd gave way slowly, and my policeman escort, with an inexplicable change of attitude, directed people to one side until we stopped at a position near the speaker's platform.

Prague Old Town Square is a cobblestoned expanse surrounded by medieval buildings. Sixty thousand people jam-packed it. Behind them, benevolent fourteenth-century Tyn Cathedral lifted its conical towers skyward. Near the center dozens of women and girls in Czech national costume stood and sat on the memorial to Jan Huss, the fourteenth-century religious heretic. Their colorful flowers and peasant dresses mantled the gray stones of the austere pedestal into a floral bower.

The crowd faced Old Town Hall, its walls blackened and gutted in fighting with the Nazis. From the upper windows hung two portraits thirty feet high. One was of Benes, the other of Stalin. Between them was draped a long banner lettered in two lines, *Long live Marshall Stalin; Prague welcomes President Benes.* Below this was the speaker's platform, and in a cleared area in front sat Czech dignitaries, flanked by Russian army brass. President and Mrs. Benes sat in the front row.

A speaker finished his introduction and President Benes walked to the platform. While he arranged his papers upon the lectern, the people welcomed him uproariously. They waved thousands of small flags, long banners fluttered, and the screams of the women on the Huss monument added a strident tone to the clamor. He nodded his head occasionally in acknowledgment, waiting for the demonstration to end, and as the noise abated an expectant quietness possessed the throng. He commenced to speak—his voice strong, positive in phrasing, and confident in inflection. The public address system was excellent, and his words filled the town square with pervasive dominance.

As his speech progressed, local sections of the crowd found occasion to respond to portions of his speech by shouting slogans in unison. Their cheerleaders led them in rhythmic chanting, ending with the climactic repetition, "President Benes! President Benes! President Benes!"

In another section of the crowd the leftists also changed slogans, competing with the first group like opposing sections at a college football game. Their rhythmic cheering also ended with three big ones, shrieked with shrill emphasis, "Premier Stalin! Premier Stalin! Premier Stalin!" They continued their rivalry at appropriate pauses throughout his address. Benes interrupted neither faction, not allowing the chanting to distract from the positive continuity of his delivery. The general ovation was generous when he finished, and he descended from the platform to be congratulated by his colleagues.

The crowd began to break up as Harry dismantled his equipment, passing down the sections to us into the truck. Our passengers left, Captain Monflein disappeared into the crowd, and Mr. Sima shook hands with us after he conferred briefly with Harry. We returned to Fred's apartment past throngs of people hurrying home to lunch.

While we ate, a radio across the street blared a recording of the parade, the tumultuous shouting echoing between the buildings and assailing us through the open windows. Fred answered a knock on the door, conversed for a few minutes, returned, and exclaimed excitedly to Harry, "My neighbor has said that on Radio Prague has come an announcement for Sergeant Downard to return to Pilsen with the film he has made." Harry looked startled and exclaimed, "Anything more than that, any details?" "No," replied Fred, "only that you were to return to Pilsen with your film as soon as possible." "Sounds like Lieutenant Melkel getting excited," mused Harry. "We'll go back tomorrow." He paused and continued, "Mr. Sima told me to go to the Hradcany Castle at three o'clock this afternoon. We might have an apointment with President Benes." We reflected upon this with no comment, subdued by the tumultuous events we had just experienced.

It was early in the afternoon when we crossed the river on the Charles Bridge and drove up the cobblestone street to the palace. The road was steep, narrow, and picturesquely curved between old buildings. Our instructions were to pass the huge, ornate gates at the front entrance, now locked and unattended, and to seek entrance far around at the side. Following a lane through a formal garden lined with a row of trees, we came to a gate behind which stood one man. As we approached he swung the gate open, shutting it behind us as we passed through. Standing on the running board, unspoken and unsmiling, he pointed the way. We passed in front of the Saint Vitus Cathedral and into a courtyard, halting in front of an entrance above which were four flags. An American and a British flag were in the cluster that included the Czech and Russian. The passageway between the buildings we had come through and the courtyard were almost empty of people, only one or two walking hastily upon silent errands.

"Not much of a crowd to welcome a president home after seven years," said Harry. We alighted and our silent guide led us into the entrance and up a thickly carpeted stairway, wide and spacious, with a marble balustrade curving to the floor above. There our boots clacked harshly on the parquet floor of the highly polished hallway lined with eighteenth-century paintings in ornate, gilded frames. We passed through rooms whose high windows, flanked with richly brocaded drapery, offered us tantalizing glimpses of the city and the river.

We stopped in a large room, whose arched ceiling and glass chandeliers were reflected in one wall, mirrored from end to end and floor to cornice. Along it were several tables, to where Harry was led and his identification card examined. Meanwhile Warren and I went back to the truck and brought up the equipment. Our truck was alone in the courtyard, and on our return through the rooms and hallways we saw no one.

Harry chose a location by a large, rounded desk near a window. He set up his camera as I helped Warren string his cable. They tested the sound. Harry made a last precautionary check and informed our guide that we were ready.

In a few minutes a door at the far end opened, and President Benes entered, followed by two secretaries. He walked over to the microphone and waited patiently while Harry framed and focused the scene in his viewfinder.

Benes carried an air of sturdy integrity about him at close range, an inner robustness that belied his small stature. His complexion was ruddy, whereas it had been pale during the day, and if he was fatigued, it was concealed.

Harry, craftsman that he was, took sufficient time to make sure his adjustments were right, and President Benes waited with relaxed self-possession. With camera ready he signaled the president, who commenced to speak. His voice was as firm and strong as during his speech in the morning. Reading from a prepared text, he spoke for about five minutes. He related the democratic traditions of Czechoslovakia and expressed desire for renewed friendship with America and the Allies. His English pronunciation was clear and intelligible.

Waiting until the camera stopped he approached us and shook hands with Warren, who said with sincere formality, "It is an honor, Sir." Harry and I thanked him for the interview as we in turn shook his hand. Looking at us appraisingly he said, "Do you believe me now about the wickedness and aggression of the Nazis? In 1935 I told many people that was the intention of the Germans, but none would listen to me. Colonel Lindbergh stood right where you are standing now," nodding his head at our feet, "and he would not believe me." His face flushed slightly as he added feelingly, "He was stupid, stupid."

"Sir," I proffered, "I heard Jan Masaryk speak in 1939 at a university in America where I was a student. It is regrettable that we did not comprehend his warning of the Nazi threat to Europe." "Yes," he replied, "I spoke to many universities in America, and I shall never forget the kindness shown to me in your country." He paused reflectively for a moment, then asked if there was anything more that we wanted. I asked him if he would sit at his desk and photographed him there, then he shook hands with us again and was rejoined by his secretaries as he left the room.

We watched the small, doughty man in silence as the door closed behind him. His audience in the morning had numbered thousands of his countrymen. He had concluded a private speech with three GIs in clandestine circumstances. We were obscure technicians, but the camera we served was vital. For him it opened a small window into the free world. We shared the cumulative feeling of the empty courtyards, the vacant corridors, the furtive gateway, underscored by the honor of this meeting with a lonely man.

Harry broke the thread of musing that gripped us by disassembling his camera. We packed our equipment and carried it out of the room and down the corridors, unaccompanied. Our guide met us at the truck and rode with us through the deserted palace yard. The late afternoon sun was well below the buildings, and the sound of our vehicle echoed noisily in the shadowy passageways. Saint Vitus Cathedral was footed in shadow, but above the sunlight struck the towers in mellow coloring. At the side gate our escort let us through, and without a word or gesture shut it behind us. In silence we drove out through the dusk beneath the trees and onto the street.

The next morning we left Prague, and the drive back to Pilsen was uneventful. The guards at the line of demarcation recognized us and waved us through. Harry took the film to Third Army headquarters, while I remained in Pilsen.

The film was exhibited in theaters in America. The extinguishing of the democratic institutions in Czechoslovakia is history. The window to the free world was a small one. It gradually closed with the death of President Benes. It was locked tightly with the tragic death of his successor, Jan Masaryk.

—Sergeant Ralph Butterfield

Sgt. Ralph Butterfield

PRESIDENT BENES walked slowly from the dark entrance of the station and paused momentarily in the brilliant sunlight. He was immediately surrounded by dignitaries and the press.

[OVERLEAF]

SIXTY THOUSAND PEOPLE jam-packed Prague Old Town Square. Dozens of women and girls in Czech national costume stood or sat on the memorial to Jan Huss—their colorful flowers and peasant dresses mantling the gray stones of the austere pedestal into a floral bower.

Sgt. Ralph Butterfield

Sgt. Ralph Butterf

"HE COMMENCED TO SPEAK—his voice strong, positive in phrasing, and confident in inflections. The public address system was excellent, and his words filled the town square with pervasive dominance."